LEARNING DISABILITIES AND BRAIN DYSFUNCTION

LEARNING DISABILITIES AND BRAIN DYSFUNCTION

An Introduction for Educators and Parents

By

CHARLES J. GOLDEN, Ph.D.
University of Nebraska Medical Center
Omaha, Nebraska

and

SANDRA ANDERSON
University of South Dakota
Vermillion, South Dakota

CHARLES C THOMAS · PUBLISHER
Springfield · Illinois · U.S.A.

Published and Distributed Throughout the World by
CHARLES C THOMAS • PUBLISHER
BANNERSTONE HOUSE
301-327 East Lawrence Avenue, Springfield, Illinois, U.S.A.

© *1979, by* CHARLES C THOMAS • PUBLISHER
ISBN 0-398-03861-9
Library of Congress Catalog Card Number: 78-13251

With THOMAS BOOKS *careful attention is given to all details of
manufacturing and design. It is the Publisher's desire to present
books that are satisfactory as to their physical qualities and artistic
possibilities and appropriate for their particular use.* THOMAS
BOOKS *will be true to those laws of quality that assure a good
name and good will.*

Printed in the United States of America
N-11

Library of Congress Cataloging in Publication Data

Golden, Charles J., 1949-
    Learning disabilities and brain dysfunction.

    Bibliography: p. 144
    Includes index.
    1. Brain-damaged children. 2. Learning disabilities. 3. Neuropsy-
chology. I. Anderson, Sandra, joint author. II. Title.
RJ496.B7G64   618.9'28'5884   78-13251
ISBN 0-398-03861-9

PREFACE

THE AREA of learning disabilities has engendered significant interest among the public and among the professionals in the medical and behavioral sciences. This interest has led to a plethora of theories on the etiology and treatment of these disabilities. Theories have suggested developmental lags, emotional difficulties, perceptual impairments, genetic disorders, ophthamological disturbances, auditory losses, or some combination of nutritional problems ranging from multivitamin loss to food additive allergies. As yet, no therapy has shown itself to account for the problems in all learning disabled children.

This state of affairs has convinced many psychologists and educators that there is more than one cause of learning disabilities. We are discussing a large group of very different youngsters when we use the term learning disabilities; thus, any generalizations we make are likely to be wrong because LD children are different from one another. The recognition of the differences between children clearly calls for us to focus our research and studies on each group of LD children separately. In this way, we can endeavor to ensure each individual child an optimal diagnostic and treatment approach.

The present volume is an attempt to summarize for the interested educator and parent the modern research in neuropsychology, the study of the relationship between behavior and brain function. In particular, it is an attempt to present what theories, diagnostic approaches, and rehabilitation ideas developed in neuropsychology can be applied successfully and effectively to the group of learning disabled children who are brain damaged. As the research in the initial chapters will suggest, this is a significantly large subgroup among learning disabled children, although the exact size differs depending on whom one chooses to believe.

It is hoped that the reader may come to recognize that the

brain injured, learning disabled child cannot be easily categorized. The idea that these children have several basic symptoms in common arises out of a misunderstanding about brain damage, not modern research on the subject. The symptoms a child may show can differ enormously from child to child depending on a variety of factors discussed in the first nine chapters.

This view of the brain damaged, learning disabled child is based on modern neuropsychological theory. In addition, the meaning of these theories for diagnosing children will be described, as well as the implications for rehabilitation programming. We wish to show that no diagnostic program or rehabilitation technique or set of techniques is right for every child: our interest must be in the individual child rather than groups of children. For this reason, we have avoided giving the reader *the* diagnostic sign, *the* test, *the* rehabilitation program which will solve the child's problem, as no such simple answer exists. Such answers only serve to distort the child's real problems and to insure less than maximal treatment.

Instead, we will try to convey an appreciation and understanding of the complexity of the brain and the brain injured child, presented in such a way that the reader need only be interested and intelligent rather than an expert in medicine or physiology. We strongly believe that this basic understanding will enable the educator and layperson to better understand brain injured, learning disabled children, the first major step to seeing that these children receive maximal diagnostic and rehabilitation opportunities.

CONTENTS

LEARNING DISABILITIES AND BRAIN DYSFUNCTION

Section I
PRELIMINARY CONCERNS

Chapter 1

INTRODUCTION:
LEARNING DISABILITIES AND BRAIN
DYSFUNCTION

THE TERM *learning disabilities* refers to a wide variety of conditions in which a child or adult of normal intelligence fails to perform at an expected level in a specific intellectual area. As modern society has become more complex and as universal education for all children has been established as a right, the specific effects of learning disabilities have become more visible. As a result, there has been growing concern from parents, educators, mental health professionals, and physicians that we identify the causes of learning disabilities and the procedures necessary for their remediation.

A survey of the professional literature reveals a number of possible etiologies for learning disabilities. Theories of learning disabilities have been based on learning theory, attentional processes, ophthalmological observations, genetic disorders, emotional disturbance, perceptual processes, perceptual-motor integration, and brain function. In general, books and articles on these theories have approached the development of learning disabilities from two major viewpoints. An eclectic view encourages evaluation and treatment that encompasses a wide range of possible etiologies, while more specific views attempt to identify a single cause as the basis for all learning disabilities.

In general, the eclectic approach has been most widely accepted. This approach has resulted in the growing recognition that the individuals who are collectively called *learning disabled* comprise many different subpopulations. Each has a different etiology, and each requires different evaluation techniques and

5

remediation procedures. The eclectic approach has spurred the growth of multidisciplinary evaluations, in which a child is examined by a diagnostic team comprised of representatives of many different professions. The variety of diagnostic approaches is expected to increase the probability of correctly identifying the child's problem and referring the child to treatment by the appropriate profession or professions.

The recognition by educators and other professionals of the different subgroups summarized by the label "learning disabled" places a new and important responsibility on professionals in the field. It becomes important that a child be identified as belonging to one group or another, so the particular remediation techniques applicable to that child can be specified and implemented.

Brain Injury and Learning Disabilities

Brain injury was one of the earliest explanations for learning disorders. As early as 5000 years ago, Egyptians had observed the relationship between the brain and learning. By 500 BC, Pythagoras had identified the brain as the seat of intellect. During the later nineteenth century, Morgan (1896) observed that dyslexia (inability to read) in brain injured adults was similar to dyslexia in children, whom we would today consider learning disabled. Hinshelwood (1917) suggested that the disorder was due to improper development of brain centers dealing with visual memory, as did several other investigators (Penn, 1966). During the 1960s the relationship of brain injury to learning disorders was firmly established by the popularity of the term *minimal cerebral dysfunction* (Mercer, Forgnone, and Wolking, 1976; Clements, 1966).

Despite a long history of extensive investigation, the brain injury hypothesis has been among the most controversial and most misunderstood of all explanations for learning disabilities. The term itself evokes fears that the condition is an untreatable problem or the concern only of physicians or physiologists. To others the label brain damage may suggest the severely impaired mentally retarded child, rather than the learning disabled child with normal intelligence and a specific, limited disability. Conflicting statement from experts in education, psychology, and medicine regarding the effects of brain damage have further contributed to the misunderstandings about brain injury and its relationship to learning disabilities.

Reasons for the Controversy and Misunderstandings

There have been a number of important reasons for the brain injury controversy in learning disabilities. One factor has been the relatively undeveloped state of the field of neuropsychology, the study of the relationship between the brain and behavior. Although the brain has been recognized as the seat of the intellect for over 5000 years, most attempts at understanding brain function have met with failure. In the last century, thoughts about brain function began to crystallize as two major theories came to dominate the field. The localizationist theory held that each area in the brain controlled a specific skill. Thus, injury to a specific part of the brain would cause dyslexia, the inability to read, while injury to another part of the brain would cause dysgraphia, the inability to write. However, the failure of this theory to predict many deficits shown by real patients caused physicians and psychologists to question its accuracy.

The second theory, that of equipotentiality, suggested that all higher thinking skills were dependent on the brain as a whole. What mattered was not the location of the injury, but rather the percentage of the brain that was injured. The higher the percentage, the greater the degree of disability. An important consequence of this theory was the assumption that the only difference in symptoms of different brain injured patients lay in the degree of disability. All brain injury individuals would be expected to have many characteristics in common, while differences would be attributed only to differences in the severity of injury.

This latter conclusion led to one of the myths commonly held within the field of brain function: all brain injured children are essentially alike. In actual practice, brain injured children differ from one another as much as normal children do. There are no symptoms which all brain injured children have in common with one another. Consequently there is no one treatment program, or even a limited set of programs that is applicable to all, or even most, brain injured children.

The belief that all brain injured children are essentially alike had lead many to conclude, erroneously, that a given child could not be brain injured because he or she did not exhibit any of the "classical" symptoms of brain injury, such as poor attention span, hyperactivity, and emotional problems. It also led many lay people as well as professionals to conceive of the brain injured child in a stereotyped manner.

The clash of alternative theories about brain function has served to further confuse issues concerning the relationship of brain injury to learning disabilities. In many cases, statements have been based more on theoretical views than on hard empirical evidence. The variety of positions held by different "experts" has often been confusing and difficult to understand. Only recently have theories linking brain injury and learning disabilities taken advantage of the modern literature on brain function, long after an inadequate view of brain function has already become deeply established.

A second major problem relating brain injury to learning disabilities is that of determining whether a given child is brain injured. The diagnosis of brain injury has traditionally been defined by the physician's critieria, through the results of the physical neurological examination plus additional tests such as the electroencephalogram (EEG). (See Chapter 2 for a description of these tests.) However, these tests were not designed to detect subtle brain dysfunction or even chronic, limited brain injury. They were devised to locate and aid in the treatment of currently harmful or life-threatening disorders. While they are able to identify some of the disorders within a learning disabled population, they also fail to detect many disorders, including cases in which brain injury is known to have occurred. Thus, while the medical examination is a necessary and important part of the evaluation of the learning disabled child suspected to have brain injury, its diagnostic conclusions cannot be considered final.

The alternative method of diagnosing the presence of brain injury has been through the use of psychological tests. However, psychological examinations have also frequently been found to be deficient (Section III). Diagnosis of brain injury in children through psychological testing is most commonly based on the results of one or two tests, e.g. the Bender-Gestalt, the Wechsler intelligence tests, or the Frostig Test. However, the performance of a child or adult on a given test is dependent on a wide variety of factors operating in the testing situation, including emotional problems, inability to work with the examiner, peripheral motor deficits, cultural problems, language problems, and motivational problems, which may obscure the person's actual ability level. As a result, the use of a small number of psychological tests as a definitive indicator of the presence or absence of brain dysfunction is a highly questionable procedure.

A related diagnostic problem is the diagnosis of learning disabilities themselves. While there are numerous definitions, most specify the existence of a specific disorder in an individual of otherwise normal intelligence, whose deficit cannot be attributed to such factors as cultural problems, mental retardation, peripheral injuries, and emotional instability. In practice, the learning disabled child may be defined as a child "two years behind grade level" who has a normal intelligence.

Problems in the Learning Disabilities Literature

Three enduring problems have continued to impede progress in the accumulation of knowledge about learning disabilities and have contributed to the development of inconsistencies in the literature. The first problem, briefly discussed earlier in the chapter, is the definition of learning disabilities. Before we can determine whether learning disabled children are neurologically impaired, we must be able reliably to identify the learning disabled child. The problem of the definitional criteria of learning disabilities creates difficulty in the selection of children to be included in research. Differences in definition, with inclusion criteria often inadequately specified, make difficult the evaluation or comparison of research results and the achievement of comparability in the samples of children in the various studies. Thus, it cannot be determined whether a given sample of learning disabled children is representative of the whole population of children labeled as learning disabled.

In most studies, the definition of learning disabilities is based on some practical consideration, which can lead to bias in the composition of the group of learning disabled children. A children's mental health clinic might include in the population of learning disabled children all children referred to the clinic who have learning problems but who are not retarded and do not show serious emotional problems. A neurologist might define the population as all children referred for a neurological examination because they cannot read or who are awkward or hyperactive. The school psychologist might consider as learning disabled all children with normal IQ who do poorly on achievement tests.

Groups of learning disabled children recruited through a variety of referral sources might form fairly representative samples, since referrals may come from many sources which do not influence one another. However, when referrals come only from one referral source or when investigators employ idiosyncratic criteria for inclusion of a child within the group of learning disabled children, the collection of subjects might be more biased. One study, for example, may disqualify all children with a history of brain damage and then later conclude that learning disabled children show no signs of brain damage. Another study may only include children considered by the author as learning disabled, a clear invitation to experimenter bias in which the experimenter, consciously or unconsciously, chooses children who fit the hypothesis the experimenter wishes to prove. Finally, studies obtaining subjects from one referral source may have a nonrepresentative group of children from which to attempt to draw inferences. Thus, it is important to compare the results from different laboratories, since consistent results from a given laboratory or research team may be the result of consistent bias in the students at that setting. When similar conclusions can be reached from the findings of many independent laboratories, they can more comfortably be considered reliable.

Advantages of a Brain Injury Theory

Despite the controversy that surrounds the brain injury hypothesis, several factors make it an attractive explanation for many forms of learning disabilities. The most obvious reason is the recognition that learning does take place in the brain. Proponents of the brain injury theory can convincingly argue that many alternative theories of the etiology of learning disabilities (for example, perceptual deficit, maturational lag) may only be special cases of brain dysfunction. Thus, the brain dysfunction theory may offer the possibility of integrating many apparently diverse etiological theories, which may in turn lead to a simplification of diagnosis and new integrated approaches to rehabilitation planning.

A second, related advantage is the possibility that brain dysfunction theories might identify a single deficit as the cause of a myriad of seemingly unrelated symptoms in the learning disabled child. As we shall see in our discussion of brain function, under certain conditions isolated, limited injuries can produce patterns of deficits which, while appearing at first to be unrelated, have a common etiology. This common etiology may offer a common remediational approach.

A third virtue is the growing recognition that properly diagnosed brain injuries offer ample rehabilitation possibilities (Luria, 1963, 1970; Golden, 1976, 1978). Theories of brain dysfunction, combined with our growing empirical knowledge of the effects of brain injury, increasingly enable the clinician to specify individualized remediation programs that can maximally develop a child's potential.

Fourth, the evidence indicates that some learning disabled children (the number depending upon the specific definition of brain injury and learning disabilities) are indeed brain injured and that many children with limited brain injuries meet the defining characteristics of learning disabilities. For these individuals at least, the brain injury hypothesis offers an understanding of the disability, something which can be invaluable for the parent, educator, or friend.

Summary

The learning disabilities literature has recognized that learning disabilities may result from a number of different processes. One of the major causes which has been suggested for learning disabilities is brain dysfunction. This hypothesis has been highly controversial because of differences over what constitutes brain damage, the effects of brain damage, and the determination of who is and who is not brain damaged. Another problem in establishing the relationship between brain injury and the etiology of learning disabilities is the definition of learning disabilities.

Despite the controversy, there are a number of reasons for accepting a brain injury etiology for at least part of the learning disabled population. These advantages include the theoretical relationship between brain function and behavior, the possibility of integrating diverse etiologies, the ability to integrate a series of seemingly unrelated symptoms, and the advantages of the rehabilitation planning based on work with limited brain injuries.

Chapter 2

MEDICAL EVIDENCE

O NE OF THE main sources of evidence relating brain injury and learning disabilities comes from medical research. Many of these studies were generated by the observation that disorders seen in learning disabled children are nearly identical to the disorders seen in brain damaged adults and children. The evidence that has been gathered falls into three broad categories: (1) results of EEG studies; (2) results of physical neurological examinations; and (3) results suggesting a genetic basis to learning disabilities.

EEG Research

The electroencephalogram (EEG) records measurements of the frequency and voltage of the electrical potentials caused by activity in brain tissue at the surface of the brain. In most EEG studies, electrodes are placed on the scalp in a pattern across the skull. Readings may be taken both while the subject is asleep and awake as these conditions may yield different patterns.

Extensive experience with EEGs has enabled neurologists and other physicians to establish, within limits, the normal patterns of electrical activity in the brain as measured by the EEG. These patterns differ depending on the age of the subject and other parameters which may be taken into account when reading (interpreting) the EEG. It has generally been found that up to 15 or 20 percent or the normal population will show "abnormal" patterns on the EEG (Mayo Clinic, 1976).

There are substantial questions about the effectiveness of the EEG as a diagnostic instrument in learning disabilities. In cases of known brain dysfunction, only about 50 percent will actually be identified (Filskov and Goldstein, 1974). Thus negative readings on the EEG, i.e. the lack of any noticeable abnormalities, do not necessarily indicate an intact brain, only one that shows no EEG abnormalities. Consequently, results of EEG studies may seriously underestimate the actual percentage of brain abnormalities in a population.

While the EEG may be questionable in diagnosing individual cases, it does offer a test of the hypothesis about learning disabilities and brain dysfunction. While it would not be expected that every child with a brain abnormality would show positive EEG findings, we would expect EEGs of groups of learning disabled children to show significantly more abnormalities than groups of nonlearning disabled children if the brain injury hypothesis is true. The results of the EEG research may give us a lower limit for the number of learning disabled children who show signs of brain dysfunction.

Numerous studies have examined EEG functions in learning disabled and brain damaged children (Ayers and Torres, 1967; Benton and Bird, 1963; Clements and Peters, 1962; Laufer, Denhoff, and Solomon, 1957; Muehl, Knott, and Benton, 1965; Oettinger, Nekonishi, and Gill, 1967; Wikler, Dixon, and Parker, 1970). The studies have all agreed that there are few signs of active seizure activity in learning disabled children.

Studies differ, however, on the percentage of learning disabled children who show EEG patterns which differ from normal EEG patterns. Daryn (1960) reported a 40 percent rate of EEG abnormalities in his study, while Cohn (1961) reported 50 percent. Muehl, Knott, and Benton (1965) identified a 63 percent rate. Hughes, Leander, and Ketchum (1949) found a rate of 75 percent, while Capute, Niedermeyer, and Richardson (1968) found a 50 percent rate. An overall evaluation of these studies suggested that the incidence of abnormal EEGs in the learning disabled population was about 60 percent compared to a 20 percent or less rate in the control (normal) children.

Penn (1966) concluded that 70 to 75 percent of children with specific reading disorders had abnormal EEGs compared to a 5 or 10 percent rate in the applicable control populations, as did Kennard, Rabinowitch, and Wexler (1952). Penn also stated that there was no difference in the rates of EEG abnormalities in populations of children with reading problems resulting from a birth injury and those known to have acquired the deficits later, after a confirmed brain injury.

Although this data clearly suggests that there is at least a subpopulation of learning disabled children who show EEG abnormalities, it must be recognized that this correlation does not prove that the EEG abnormalities are related to the learning disabilities. (In fact, there is no way to directly prove this unless we did an experiment which deliberately inflicted EEG abnormalities onto otherwise normal children.) It must also be remembered that it is possible to find groups of learning disabled children who would show no EEG abnormalities whatsoever. Despite these limitations, however, it appears that the evidence to date justifies a tentative conclusion that some learning disabled children may show significant brain dysfunction. This population may include up to or more than half of all children identified as learning disabled.

The Physical Neurological Examination

The second most frequently investigated neurological measure in learning disabled children is the physical neurological examination. This examination consists of tests of cranial nerve function (sight, smell, eye movements, tongue movements, facial sensation, audition, balance) ; tests of reflexes, primarily involving the arms and legs; tests of cerebellar function (placing finger to nose with and without eyes closed, coordination) ; tests of motor and sensory function throughout the body, including sensitivity to temperature, vibration, touch, and pain; and tests of general cerebral function, including emotional responsiveness, memory, social skills, and intelligence.

Like the EEG, the physical neurological examination has some serious drawbacks in identifying learning disabled children. A primary problem is the lack of standardization of the neurological examination. While some physicians will include a detailed evaluation of all the areas cited above, many will do only some of the tests. The procedures used depend on the physician's orientation and confidence in the various measures, as well as such factors as the source of the physician's training, time allowed for the examination, and cooperation of the child. Thus, differences in results can often be attributed to differences in the neurological functions examined.

A second, related problem is the lack of standards of what constitutes an "abnormal" response. Normal individuals may vary considerably on tests of neurological function; consequently, the decision as to what constitutes an indication of a possible disorder is highly subjective. The accuracy of an examination is highly dependent on the skill and experience of the individual physician.

Another significant problem involves the meaning of *soft signs*. These signs are uncertain in meaning, because while they do occur in individuals with brain injury, they also occur fairly frequently in groups of individuals without any impairment. Unfortunately, these soft signs are often the only symptoms present in the learning disabled child. The *hard signs* that are given more credence by neurologists are better at detecting current acute disorders such as recent head trauma, tumors, or serious structural damage to the brain than the limited deficits which are postulated in learning disabled children. Hence, the emphasis a neurologist places on soft signs can cause different physicians to reach diametrically opposite conclusions in the case of an individual child. Even the presence or absence of hard signs does not give an unequivocal answer in either direction when dealing with the individual child.

Hertzig, Bortner, and Birch (1969) did an extensive examination of ninety children educationally designated as "minimal brain dysfunction" (learning disabled), comparing them to fifteen children educationally labeled as normal. The authors found that 29 percent of the learning disabled children showed hard signs of neurological impairment. In all cases, these hard signs were generally motor movements impaired more on one side of the body when compared to the other. All the deficits were slight, and none would be considered striking or immediately obvious to observers. No child in the normal group had any of these signs.

When looking at the soft signs, the authors found that 90 percent of the learning disabled children showed significant soft signs. About 23 percent of these children were the same ones who also had hard signs, leaving 6 percent of the children with hard signs showing no soft signs. About 66 percent of the children had soft signs without any hard signs. Overall, 94 percent of the children (85 of 90) had some neurological abnormality.

The most frequently occurring soft signs were problems with balance, coordination, and speech. Less frequent, but still occurring in a large number of children, were abnormalities in responding to double simultaneous tactile stimulation (reporting only one touch when actually being touched twice), disorders of muscle tone and indications of overflow movements. Of the ninety learning disabled children, nineteen were classified as hyperkinetic. The authors found more soft signs in the hyperkinetic children than the remaining learning disabled patients.

From these results, the authors concluded that learning disabled children do show higher incidences of neurological dysfunction. However, the authors emphasized that the indications of neurological dysfunction varied considerably. This study serves to point out that even within a group of learning disabled children with signs of neurological dysfunction, the children differ considerably from one another.

In a major study on the physical neurological examination, Peters, Romine, and Dykman (1975) described a large number of neurological signs which differentiate learning disabled and control children. This list included holding arms out straight, rotation of the head, the copying of finger movements, abnormal motor movements, hopping on one foot, standing on one foot, walking a straight line, foot tapping, placing a finger on one's nose with eyes closed, bilateral coordinated movements, reflexes, right-left confusion, eye movements, discrimination of two points placed on the skin, tongue movements, and a variety of reading, spelling, and writing problems.

Similar findings of an abnormal neurological examination have been found in a number of other studies as well (Clements and Peters, 1962; Ingram, 1973; Wikler, Dixon, and Parker, 1970; Penn, 1966). The conclusions from these studies have been consistent with those discussed above in suggesting a relationship between learning disabilities and brain dysfunction.

HISTORY. A significant part of the neurological examination is the history. It would be expected that learning disabled children should show more signs of conditions that can cause brain injury, e.g. difficult birth or anoxia. In addition, children with a history of possible brain injury should show higher incidences of learning disabilities than children without such a history.

Kawi and Pasamanick (1958) found that one out of every six of 205 learning disabled boys had histories suggesting significant maternal complications in pregnancy, as compared to a rate of only 1.5 percent (1 in 67) in matched control children. These complications included such problems as hypertension and other conditions which can lead to fetal anoxia, a deficit in the oxygen supply available to the fetus.

Lucas, Rodin, and Simson (1965), using educational referrals, studied seventy-two children likely to be learning disabled. Extensive neurological examinations and histories were completed on each child. They found that children with a history of birth difficulty also showed signs of brain impairment such as abnormal reflexes, a history of walking late, and other neurological problems. Children whose mothers had a "difficult pregnancy" were found to show impairment on hopping on one leg and impairment of rapid bilateral movements. These children were also more likely to be judged by physicians as showing an overall abnormal neurological examination. The authors also reported that hyperactivity was often associated with an overall abnormal examination. Wikler, Dixon, and Parker (1970) reported that the number of neurological signs seen in learning disabled children was highly related to the child's birth weight. The authors suggested that this may indicate that premature babies, who are more susceptible to brain damage, are also more likely to develop learning disabilities.

Genetic Theories of Brain Dysfunction

The third major line of research implicating brain injury in children has come from genetic research. Genetic theories basically argue that many learning disabilities result from deficiencies in chemical pathways in the brain which are the result of hereditary factors. In general, the proof for the genetic theory has been less extensive and less impressive than the research from the first two approaches discussed here. One of the reasons for this has been the difficulty and complexity of collecting sufficient genetic data.

McGlannan (1968) attempted to study genetic influences in three generations of sixty-five families, each of which contained at least one child designated as "reading disabled." Each reading disabled child was also screened for uncorrected peripheral disorders, e.g. poor vision, obvious organicity, and evidence of neurotic or psychopathic behavior. All the children scored above 90 on the Wechsler Intelligence Scale for Children. Most subjects were found to exhibit disorders of laterality, maturational lag, inability to perform under stress, finger identification problems, touch localization errors, and poor fine motor coordination.

McGlannan found a higher rate of twinning in the selected population than in the normal population (68% of the families in three generations, almost three times as high as would be expected). He reported that there was a greater than normal rate of reading disabilities in the siblings of twins, suggesting that these families were more "vulnerable" to learning disabilities. The author suggested that this vulnerability may be related to biochemical disorders which may also be related to the high rates of allergies.

One problem with such studies is the interaction of genetic and environmental influence. While the children in a single family had a common genetic background, they also had a common emotional, physical, and intellectual environment which could be the cause for higher rates of learning disabilities. There could also be factors which made it more likely for children in these families to suffer birth trauma or other disorders of pregnancy, factors which may be genetically related. Thus, the higher incidence of reading disabilities could be the secondary result of a genetic disorder rather than the primary effect.

Rossi (1972) has argued that many of these learning disabilities result from a developmental lag in basic processes of the brain caused by a biochemical, genetically inherited deficiency. Kalat (1976), as well as other researchers, has argued that dopamine deficiencies in the brain may cause hyperactivity in learning disabled children. The researchers have demonstrated "similar" effects in rats in which dopamine deficiency was induced by experimental means (Kalat, 1976; Shaywitz, 1976). Although this research suggests that such a biochemical deficiency can be a possible cause of learning disabilities (or the rat equivalent), this does not constitute proof that any brain disorder in the learning disabled child is either biochemically related or genetically inherited. More research is needed in this area before any conclusions can be reached.

Summary

The evidence from the medical literature suggesting brain injury as a cause of learning disabilities is briefly reviewed in this chapter. The presence of a high number of abnormal EEGs in learning disabled children was documented, as well as the limitations of such a finding. Results of neurological examinations in learning disabled children were presented which yielded similar data. Overall, these two research areas suggest that up to 50 percent or more of learning disabled children (as picked by these studies) may show evidence of neurological abnormality. The chapter also examined some genetic theories of inherited biochemical deficiencies which may cause brain dysfunction in some learning disabled children.

Chapter 3

PSYCHOLOGICAL EVIDENCE

THE SECOND source of evidence for hypothesizing a relationship between brain injury and learning disabilities has been from psychological tests. It has been recognized for centuries that psychological deficits in behavior are one of the major effects of brain injuries, especially those injuries that involve the cerebral hemispheres which make up most of the brain in humans. Psychological tests are especially useful in diagnosing limited brain injuries which do not show marked motor or sensory deficits, the type of brain injury most often theoretically associated with learning disabilities.

Although there has long been agreement that psychological skills are affected by brain injury, there has been a continuing controversy on the nature of that relationship. As noted in the first chapter, two major approaches have dominated the field: the equipotential view and the localizationist view. The equipotential view has emphasized the presence of generalized deficits across all forms of brain damage, while the localizationist view has emphasized evidence which suggests impairment of one part of the brain as compared to other, intact areas of the brain. Both of these viewpoints have generated evidence supportive of the hypothesis that brain injury is linked to learning disabilities, and both forms of evidence will be evaluated in this chapter.

The approaches described in this chapter owe a great deal to the extensive contributions of Ward Halstead and Ralph Reitan (Halstead, 1947; Reitan, 1966) whose work has contributed enormously to the use of psychological tests in the clinical diagnosis of brain damage. Byron Rourke (1975), W.H. Gaddes (1968), Arthur Benton (1964), and Elizabeth Koppitz (1964, 1975), pioneers in applying neuropsychological principles and theories to learning disabilities, must also be recognized for many of the ideas and approaches presented in this chapter.

Level of Performance Approach

The most common approach to neuropsychological assessment in children and adults has been the level of performance method. This method argues that brain injured children and adults should, in general, do more poorly on psychological tests sensitive to brain injury than groups of control subjects. In clinical work, an attempt is made to set a *cut-off* point for a test. If an individual scores above a cut-off point, they are classified as normal. If a score is attained which is below the cut-off point, the subject is classified as brain injured.

This approach has several major problems. Level of performance in a given client may be down for a variety of reasons other than brain damage. These reasons may include mental retardation, emotional disorders, motivational problems, an inability to get along with an examiner, and other similar problems. Thus, a number of individuals will be falsely labeled as brain damaged by this method. On the other hand, a single test is limited in the number of skills it can evaluate. Since the effects of brain injury will differ from person to person, there may be no deficit in the skill measured by a test. This will cause a brain injured individual to be diagnosed as "normal."

Although these factors limit the value of this method in the diagnosis of the individual patient, the approach still provides a test of the relationship between brain injury and learning disabilities. However, several precautions must be taken for adequate research in this area. First, subjects suspected of emotional disorders, poor environmental or cultural backgrounds, mental retardation, poor motivation, and the like must not be included in a learning disabilities sample. Thus, we are able to obtain a group where those explanations are not important ones, leaving the hypothesis of brain injury a much more likely choice to account for any skill deficits observed. Second, it is necessary to choose test measures appropriate to the group being tested. For example, a seven-year-old child would not be given a test more appropriate for a twelve-year-old. Finally, test conditions must be optimized: there should be no distraction for the child, the examiner should be skilled and experienced in working with learning disabled children, and the examiner should not be aware of whether a child is learning disabled. This last requirement avoids experimental bias (discussed earlier) on the part of the examiner.

In general, studies attempt to meet the conditions discussed above, although it is sometimes difficult to assess the exact degree of compliance from the published report of a study. As with the neurological evidence in Chapter 2, then, we must rely more on the weight of the overall evidence rather than specific studies.

BENDER-GESTALT. Perhaps one of the most widely used level of performance indicators employed with learning disabled children is the Bender-Gestalt Test. The test is basically a measure of a child's ability to copy drawings presented by the examiner. The drawings are then scored for adequacy of reproduction, the presence of rotations in which the figures are drawn upside down or at an angle, and other indicators of performance. The child is then assigned a developmental age level which can be matched against the child's chronological age.

Extensive research has identified that brain injured and learning disabled children to poorly on the Bender-Gestalt. Successful discriminations between learning disabled and normal children have been reported by Wagner and Murray (1969), McConnell (1967), Stavrianos (1971), Koppitz (1975), and many others. This research has also established a relationship between Bender scores and encephalitis (Sabatino and Cramblett, 1968), abnormal EEGs (Koppitz, 1975), and other forms of brain injury (Koppitz, 1963).

Koppitz (1963, 1975) has emphasized that the level of performance approach using the Bender alone is not an adequate measure to diagnose brain injury in the individual child, as she has recognized the limitations of this approach with any single test.

PERFORMANCE ON OTHER INDICATORS OF BRAIN DYSFUNCTION. In addition to the research on the Bender, level of performance deficits in learning disabled children have been documented on a wide range of psychological tests. These tests have included measures of visual angle perception (O'Neill and Stanley, 1976), visual recall with auditory interference (Shipley and Jones, 1969), auditory sequencing (Ayres, 1969), right-left confusion (Ginsburg and Hartwick, 1971), naming speed (Spring and Capps, 1974), finger localization (Croxen and Lytton, 1971), perceptual-motor skills (Pyfer and Carlson, 1972), delayed auditory skills (Jack and Herbert, 1975), sensorimotor function (Hurwitz, Bibace, Wolff, and Rowbotham, 1972), auditory-visual integration (Beery, 1967; Birch and Belmont, 1964), color naming (Denckla, 1972), logical-grammatical speech understanding (Wiig and Semel, 1974), manual dexterity (Zurif and Carson, 1970), visual reaction time (Czudner and Rourke, 1970, 1972), auditory reaction time (Rourke and Czudner, 1972), and attention (Rourke, 1975).

Although some of these studies may be criticized for various research problems, the overall weight of this evidence indicates that there are clearly performance level signs of organicity in some learning disabled children. As with the neurological evidence, we are not left with an absolutely specific figure of the exact number of brain injured children in the learning disabled sample or the degree of brain injury involved across many cases.

Right and Left Body Side Performance

The human brain is organized so that the right cerebral hemisphere (right half of the brain) controls the motor movements of the left side of the body, tactile input from the left half of the body, primary auditory input from the left ear, and visual input from the left half of both eyes. Similarly, the left cerebral hemisphere is responsible for motor movement on the right side of the body, auditory input from the right ear, tactile input from the right half of the body, and visual input from the right half of both eyes.

This relationship allows for a powerful method of localizing and identifying cerebral deficits. If an injury is located in the right hemisphere, it is likely to impair motor movements or tactile, auditory, or visual input on the left side. If an injury is located in the left hemisphere, there is likely to be either right sided motor or sensory input. By comparing the performance of one side of the body against the performance on the other side, deficits can be identified which suggest a cerebral lesion.

This is a particularly useful technique because the subject's intact side can act as a control to tell the physician or psychologist what the performance of the opposite side should be. Thus, individuals who just happen to be slower or less responsive than other individuals are not penalized as they are under a level of performance approach.

The effectiveness of left-right differences has been demonstrated many times in the literature on adult and children brain damage (Reitan, 1966). In many studies, it has been shown that sensory and motor symptoms of lateralized cerebral damage are consistent with cognitive deficits. These studies associated left hemisphere injuries (right body side impairment) with verbal losses, while right hemisphere injuries (left body side) are associated with losses in nonverbal skills (spatial orientation, rhythm, pitch, sequencing) (see Golden, 1978, for a review of this literature, as well as Section II of the current book).

Similar associations of motor, sensory, and cognitive losses with learning disabilities have been demonstrated. Rourke, Yanni, McDonald, and Young (1973) found that motor and sensory findings implicating the left hemisphere were accompanied by verbal losses while motor-sensory findings implicating the right hemisphere were accompanied by nonverbal losses in ten– to 14-year-old learning disabled children. Zurif and Carson (1970) found evidence of impairment in left hemisphere auditory function associated with verbal losses, as did Bryden (1970). Guyer and Friedman (1975) found that verbally impaired learning disabled children had difficulty with left hemisphere verbal tasks as expected, but no problems with right hemisphere spatial tasks. McGrady and Olson (1970) obtained similar findings in a study using the Wechsler Intelligence Scale for Children.

In our own laboratory, we have found that about 60 percent of the children referred for learning disabilities show lateralized impairments in either motor skills, sensory skills, or both. These were generally consistent with the cognitive losses displayed by the children, although there were exceptions in children who appeared to have suffered more massive injuries early in life. These massive injuries appear to lead to a reorganization of brain functions (discussed in more detail in Section II). Other studies have reported similar results (Rourke, 1975).

Overall, the results from studies examining left and right body impairment have produced results well in keeping with data from known brain injured children and adults, further increasing the impression that learning disabled children are similar to brain injured children.

Other Psychological Evidence

PATHOGNOMONIC SIGNS. This approach uses specific signs which are rarely present in normal populations but are seen in brain injured populations as indications of brain damage. The approach is limited in that many brain injured clients will not show any pathognomonic signs. However, their presence is highly suggestive of brain injury and such signs are taken seriously in individual diagnosis.

In a children's test, the most consistent and familiar use of pathognomonic signs has been on the Bender-Gestalt. The signs on the Bender included rotation of a figure by more than forty-five degrees, a substitution of an angle for a curve in a drawing, a substitution of circles for dots, a failure to integrate the various parts of a figure, perseveration, the repetition of a single feature over and over again without stopping (such as continuing to draw a circle after the required circle is drawn). Koppitz (1964) urged the use of these signs in making diagnosis, but later decided that the signs were no more effective than the level of performance approach used with the Bender and discussed earlier. Koppitz (1963) did find, however, that significantly more pathognomonic signs are seen in learning disabled children.

The use of pathognomonic signs is not limited to the Bender, but can and has been used on a variety of tests in regular clinical use. Although there is a general impression among clinicians that these signs occur more frequently in learning disabled children, these conclusions have not been supported by any formal research to date.

PATTERN ANALYSIS. Pattern analysis offers the most powerful method of using psychological tests to identify the presence of brain dysfunction. This involves using a substantial number of psychological tests, each designed to measure some independent aspect of the child's behavior and of the function of the brain. By comparing the scores with one another and integrating the results, the clinician may find sets of test scores which indicate the presence of brain damage as well as the location and, in some cases, the cause. The use of formal pattern analysis has been best exemplified with adults, as demonstrated by Reitan (1966) and Luria (1966, 1973). Reitan (1974) has also demonstrated that pattern analysis can be equally useful in children, as have Reitan and Davison (1974). In one series of studies by Rourke and his associates (Rourke, Dietrich, and Young, 1973; Rourke and Telegdy, 1971; Rourke, Young, and Flewelling, 1971), the researchers demonstrated that similar patterns of test results are seen in learning disabled children as are seen in brain injured children. In a series of forty cases reviewed in our own laboratory, we found that thirty-one cases of learning disabilities had patterns of deficits similar to those found in known brain injured children.

Although the pattern approach is powerful, there is a limitation in this kind of research with learning disabled children. While the patterns in learning disabled children are the same, there is no way to prove that this actually confirms brain injury. However, the low likelihood of such patterns being caused by other problems argues that the probability of brain injury in these learning disabled children is high.

Summary

The current chapter reviews much of the psychological evidence suggesting that learning disabled children may be brain injured. Several alternate approaches to this problem are examined. The level of performance approach assumes that brain injured individuals will perform more poorly on tests sensitive to brain dysfunction. This approach, across many tests and studies, has confirmed that similar level of performance losses are seen in learning disabled children. The differential score approach uses the differences between the functioning of the left and right cerebral hemispheres to detect signs of brain injury. Research has demonstrated that many learning disabled children show a test performance indicating lateralized lesions, and that this performance is similar to the results found in brain injured children and adults. The pathognomonic approach looks for signs which are found in brain injured clients but not normal clients. On the Bender-Gestalt, increased pathognomonic signs have been seen in learning disabled children. Finally, the pattern approach, which uses overall relationships between sets of test scores, was discussed. It was indicated that learning disabled children are often found to show specific brain injuries by this approach. Overall, it was concluded that this data is highly supportive of the brain injury hypothesis.

Chapter 4

LEARNING DISABILITIES AND BRAIN DYSFUNCTION: SOME INITIAL CONCLUSIONS

IN THE PAST two chapters, we have evaluated a wide range of evidence examining the neurological and psychological performance of learning disabled children. In each case, the data repeatedly suggested that learning disabled children show performances highly similar to children with limited brain injuries. By itself, none of the evidence reviewed can be considered conclusive. However, the repeated findings of data suggesting the same conclusions across a wide range of studies, tests, and procedures gives strong support to the brain injury hypothesis. There is, at present, no alternate theory available which can account for the results presented in these chapters.

As suggested in Chapter 1, the conclusion that there are symptoms of brain injury in learning disabled children is not an all-encompassing one. There are a significant number of learning disabled children who show no signs, psychological or neurological, of brain injury. For these children, an alternative explanation to the hypothesis of brain injury is necessary.

The Meaning of a Label

Even if it is possible that some learning disabled children are brain injured, it can be questioned whether that knowledge is relevant to the child's treatment. Does finding an etiology for the child's deficit affect the child's education or offer insights into the rehabilitation and understanding of the child? All too often, the answer to these questions has been "No." Treatment and educational habilitation remained the same whether the diagnosis of brain injury, "minimal brain dysfunction," or one of the many similar labels could be legitimately placed on the child. As a result, the concept of minimal brain dysfunction has often been rejected as useless. To a great extent, this rejection expressed an appropriate dissatisfaction with the state of the field as it dealt with the remediation of the individual child, which in turn resulted from a failure by many to fully appreciate the implications of a diagnosis of brain injury.

Implications of the Diagnosis

The first implication of the diagnosis comes from the extensive literature on brain injury in adults and children: brain injury is no more a unitary disorder than learning disabled children are all alike. As we stated in the first chapter, the intention of the book is to aid in identifying a specific subpopulation of learning disabled children whose needs, both diagnostically and in treatment, differ from that of other learning disabled children. The research indicates that we can separate brain injured from other learning disabled children. However, brain injured, learning disabled children are themselves a mixed group. The children show considerable individual differences and need very different treatments, even when they all carry a specific label such as "reading retarded." The problem with the term "brain injury" is that there are many forms of brain injury. This form, in any child, is determined by a number of basic parameters (variables).

AGE OF THE CHILD. The developmental and chronological age of a child is an important aspect of brain injury. The child at six does not face the same kinds of demands or problems as the nine-year-old child, even if they have the exact same form of brain injury on all other parameters.

AGE AT THE TIME OF INJURY. The age at which an injury occurred is also very important in determining the effects of a brain injury. The major dimension is the developmental level of the child when the injury occurs. Early occurring injuries (before speech develops) have dramatically different effects from later injuries.

LOCATION OF INJURY. The area in which an injury occurs also strongly affects its description. Injuries in certain areas of the brain will produce extensive verbal deficits which interfere with almost all aspects of verbal learning, while others may affect verbal skills only slightly or not at all. Some injuries will have profound motor impairment associated, while others will show no impairment in observable motor skills.

EXTENT OF INJURY. Extent of injury affects an individual in two ways. First, the larger the injury the larger the number of areas and specific, basic skills which will be impaired. Second, larger injuries will result in less rehabilitation potential, as they are more likely to interfere with a reorganization of brain functions. Thus, larger injuries will intensify the behavioral effects of a lesion in a given area in the brain.

CAUSE OF THE INJURY. Different neurological processes cause injuries which vary in terms of severity of injury and the ability of the brain to recover. Thus, each disorder may produce demonstrably different results in the injured person's behavior.

PREMORBID LEVEL OF PERFORMANCE. Individuals who started out at a higher level of performance prior to an injury are more likely to show recovery to a higher level than individuals with a lower initial level of performance. Rehabilitation relies on the availability of alternative skills to supplement and substitute for those impaired through injury.

LEVEL OF COMPLEXITY OF A SKILL. The more basic the level at which a skill is impaired, the less recovery and retraining is possible. Thus, if only highly complex behavior is interrupted, a successful response to rehabilitation is more likely. If basic skills are impaired, however, it is much more difficult for the client to adapt and for the mental health or educational specialist to design an adequate rehabilitation program.

As can be seen, a large number of variables influence any given brain injury. These factors not only affect the behavioral expression of an injury but also the appropriate diagnostic approaches to the patient (which must vary considerably at times), as well as the kind of rehabilitation program which is maximally effective. Any single diagnostic test or rehabilitation technique can only be most appropriate for, at best, a small percentage of the learning disabled children with brain injury.

The complexity of evaluating and treating the brain injured, learning disabled child has a number of implications for the psychological, medical, and educational approaches. These implications affect not only the training and knowledge necessary for the professional treating of these children but the facilities and treatment personnel needed to carry out a maximally effective program. In turn, they also affect the level of knowledge and sophistication which needs to be transmitted to parents and others if they are to fully understand the child.

COMPREHENSIVENESS OF TRAINING IN BRAIN PROCESSES. The professional working with these children needs to understand fully the nature of brain function in both normal and learning disabled children. Although individuals can work with and design programs for learning disabled children without this training, simplification of children's problems into standard patterns which may be correct for some children but not for many others is an unfortunate result. Thus, a trade-off exists between the comprehensiveness of training and the full adequacy of the help given to children.

Many programs proposed for treating learning disabled children result in improvement for groups of learning disabled children as well as selected, individual children. The problem with these programs is not that they do not have successes, or that the average score does not show improvement, but that they are not appropriate for *each* child. Thus, one child may show significant improvement (above and beyond spontaneous recovery and natural developmental improvements) while another will show little improvement. Without a full understanding of brain processes, it is not possible to pick the program most correct for a given child.

It is to the credit of many teachers in this area that the child and program are often eventually matched up, through hard work, trial and error, and the learning that comes with experience and observation by a talented teacher. However, ability to match child and program at the outset would increase tremendously the time such teachers could spend with each child and the number of children seen, this yielding both increased learning and economic benefits.

FAMILIARITY WITH A WIDE RANGE OF DIAGNOSTIC INSTRUMENTS. Traditional training in psychological and educational diagnostic testing has involved the teaching of several instruments of a general nature which are then applied to all problems which come along. However, the diversity of the brain injured population and the specificity of the information needed for a practical rehabilitation program makes this an inappropriate strategy. Although the effectiveness of these traditional instruments can be increased considerably (and has been with those who have spent the time to develop these skills), they are still limited when compared to a comprehensive testing approach based on neuropsychological principles of brain function.

FAMILIARITY WITH NEUROLOGICAL DISORDERS. Increasing familiarity with neurology and neurological disorders is useful in understanding the physiological substrate of the observed behavior. A professional in the field of diagnosis and treatment of brain injured, learning disabled children needs to be able to evaluate new approaches to brain function and behavior, many of which turn out to be highly unlikely in light of current knowledge about the physiology of the brain. Such approaches may advertise an "educational theory" with the best of intention but without an understanding of brain function. Sophistication on the part of those who must deal with the brain injured child would help insure that these approaches would not be unsuspectingly inflicted in inappropriate ways on children, parents, and schools. Educational professionals and parents require adequate knowledge about brain function, diagnostic problems, and rehabilitation techniques to be able to assess the adequacy of new approaches which would result in changes to schools, children, and the community.

Summary

A review of the evidence presented in Section I clearly suggests that brain injury is a cause of learning disabilities in at least a significant minority of the children with school learning problems. This conclusion has several important implications: first, there is a need for an understanding of how the brain works and how to diagnose brain function if we are to help this class of children;

second, individuals working with these children, as well as parents and mental health professionals in general, need access to more current information on the function of the brain and its relationship to test performance; finally, a deeper understanding of the individualized factors which affect the expression of a brain injury is necessary. These factors include such parameters as the age of a child, the age when the injury occurred, the location of the injury, the extent of the injury, the cause of the injury, and the premorbid skills of the child.

Section II

BRAIN FUNCTION

Chapter 5

THE ORGANIZATION OF BEHAVIOR
IN THE BRAIN

MODERN THEORIES of neuropsychology have recognized that there are accurate elements in both the equipotential and localizationist positions which have dominated the field until recently. However, both theories fail to account for important aspects of brain operations. As a result, many neuropsychologists have chosen to search for a theory which can account for the positive points of both the equipotential and localization theories, while also accounting for those aspects of behavior which neither adequately addresses.

An Alternative Theory

Luria (1966) traces the beginnings of an alternative theory to the writings of J. Hughlings Jackson, a prominent English neurologist who wrote during the second half of the nineteenth century. In contrast to both the equipotential and localizationist theories, Jackson viewed mental abilities as being made up of a number of small, basic skills which were put together to yield a mental ability. For example, one does not have the ability to read: one has the ability to pay attention to visual material, to break this material down into isolated units, to associate these units with language parts (letters or words), to match these language parts with their auditory equivalents stored in memory, to decode these auditory equivalents, to synthesize these equivalents into words and sentences, to associate these with objects and actions, to analyze their grammatical structure, and to comprehend the meaning of what is read.

Consequently, the loss of the ability to read may be caused by the loss of many different abilities. Interruption of the process at any one of the links or the pathways that hold these links together can impair the behavior. Thus, what we call *dyslexia*, the inability to read, can represent an inability to focus on visual material, to decode the matched auditory stimuli, and so on. In fact, even more abilities than these enter into reading as this is a somewhat simplistic explanation of a highly complex process. Reading also involves, for example, skills that enable us to scan across a line sequentially, to remain on a single line and not wander onto other lines, to retain pertinent past readings in memory, to deal with abstract symbolism, and more. This depends on the type of material being read, the way it is written, the language it is written in, and other important factors.

Jackson goes on to say that the loss of a specific area within the brain will lead to the loss of one of these skills, thus making an individual unable to read. However, since these skills are distributed in locations throughout the brain, almost any injury can lead to the interruption of an ability like reading. However, the degree to which reading is impaired and the specific problems the patient shows will differ greatly, despite the fact that the patients can all be included under the term *dyslexia*.

This theory leads to two predictions. First, injuries in a specific area of the brain will cause a specific deficit such as dyslexia, as is contended by those who believe in the localizationist theory. Secondly, injuries in many different areas of the brain may cause the loss of the ability to read, as would be predicted by those who believe in an equipotential theory. Thus, Jackson's theory can account for the research results generated by both theories, making it a more comprehensive theory and a better reflection of actual brain-behavior relationships.

Alternate Representation in the Nervous System

Another important concept advanced by Jackson was the concept that the same behavior is represented in different ways in the nervous system. For example, a person with a brain injury may not be able to repeat the word "no," no matter how hard the person tried. But the same person, in frustration at being repeatedly asked to say no, may blurt out, "No, doctor, I can't say no" (Luria, 1966). While the first attempt to say no was under voluntary control, the second was under emotional control.

Luria explains this phenomenon by invoking the concept of functional systems. A functional system represents the pattern of cooperation among different areas in the brain which result in a given behavior such as speaking or reading. All behavior is the result of at least one functional system, and much human behavior may be the result of several systems. An important aspect of this theory states that there can be more than one functional system designed to accomplish the same behavior. Thus, while the sequence presented earlier can be described as the functional system for reading, one could design and teach a child an alternate way to learn to read which would produce a second functional system whose end result was reading behavior.

When brain injury exists, a functional system can be made ineffective if any of the components within it are injured. Thus, one can conceive of a functional system as a chain: If any link is broken, the chain is no longer effective. However, if a second functional system is available, the individual may show no deficit. Thus, if there are two functional systems available for reading within a given individual, an injury which interrupted only one of them would not interfere with the individual's ability to read. Thus, it might appear, on the surface at least, that the brain injury had no effect.

Each area in the brain may, and usually does, take part in more than one functional system. As a consequence, the injury of any single area within the brain will affect several functional systems. If one can analyze precisely which functional systems have been affected, one can identify the location of the injury. However, knowing that a given functional system, reading, is injured is not sufficient information to determine the location or extent or nature of a brain injury. This can only come with a comprehensive evaluation of all functional systems so that the pattern of functional systems impairment may be determined.

Major Units of the Brain

Luria (1966) has identified three major units of the brain whose intercooperation is necessary in nearly every functional system, although different parts of each unit may be involved in a given behavior.

FIRST UNIT. The first unit of the brain is involved in attention and arousal. This system alerts various parts of the brain that there are stimuli which must be attended to and raises the arousal level of those areas which are to receive the stimulation. This system is heavily involved in emotional response to stimuli, as well as in our overall level of activity. Although this system is among the most difficult to study in man, it is also among the most important in such behaviors as hyperactivity and over-emotionality. The system is located in the brain stem and limbic system and represents very old structures of the brain (see illustration).

SECOND UNIT. The second unit is responsible for sensory integration and input. This unit receives, via nerve impulses from the sensory organs, the stimuli for vision, hearing, and touch. It is the responsibility of the second unit to integrate these basic impulses into understandable configurations. Although some of this integration is inborn, most of it is learned. Thus we learn to hear and integrate certain sounds into speech units (phonemes).

In addition to making input from an individual sense meaningful, the second unit is also responsible for integrating input from different senses: thus it integrates tactile, auditory, and visual input. This extremely significant function plays an important role in speech, reading, writing, and other major intellectual skills. The second unit is located in the back (posterior) half of the cerebral hemispheres.

THIRD UNIT. The third unit is responsible for planning, decision making, evaluation of behavior, and the direction of observable behavior. This unit makes decisions on the performance behavior based on the integrated information fed to it by the second unit and on memory. It is responsible for turning intentions into motor behavior and for organizing the sequences of gross and fine motor behavior. Finally, it is responsible for the evaluation of

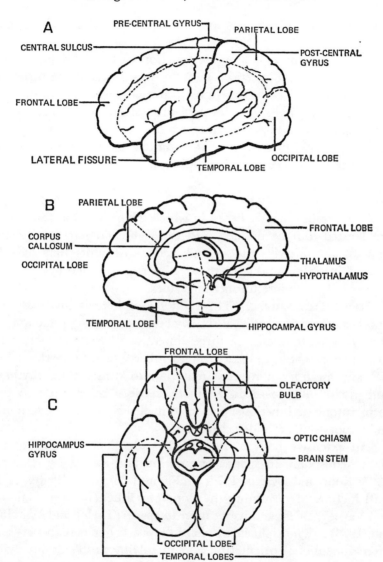

Structure of the brain from three angles. A looks at the brain from a lateral (side) view. B looks at the inside of the brain after cutting it in half by dividing the left and right hemispheres. C shows the view of the brain from below. The first functional unit is located in the depths of B (where the thalamus is indicated) and in the lower surface displayed in C. The second functional unit can be seen in the right halves of A and B (labeled temporal, occipital, and parietal lobes). The third functional unit (labeled frontal lobes) is most clearly seen in A.

what is done, constantly monitoring and making changes as necessary.

An important aspect of the function of the third unit is the large number of connections between this unit and the first unit. The first unit affects and controls arousal levels, attention, and emotionality. Thus, our level of arousal and emotional activation can affect and heavily influence the function of any decisions made by the third unit. The third unit is located in the anterior (front) half of the cerebral hemispheres.

Hemispheric Differences

The cerebral hemispheres, in which the second and third units are located, can be divided into the right and left hemispheres (halves). Similarly, the second and third units may also be divided into right and left halves. The right and left hemispheres appear to have different functional roles.

RIGHT HEMISPHERE. The right hemisphere is involved in a number of major nonverbal skills. Foremost among these are the ability to locate oneself in three-dimensional space; to work with spatial coordinates; to draw; to remember visual, nonverbal material and auditory nonverbal material; to demonstrate rhythmic and pitch abilities; to discriminate between color hues; to perform automatic functions; and to control the left body side motor and sensory skills (Golden, 1978).

An extensive body of research has identified the role of the right hemisphere in spatial orientation and awareness (Benton, 1967; Kohn and Dennis, 1974; McFie and Zangwill, 1960). This skill includes determining the slope of a line (Benton, Hannay, and Varney, 1975) and its location in space (Taylor and Warrington, 1973). The right hemisphere plays a major part in two- and three-dimensional orientation and in solving problems involving spatial reasoning (Benton and Fogel, 1962; McFie, 1970; Zaidel and Sperry, 1973).

The ability to recognize faces has been associated with right hemisphere function (Benton, Levin, and Van Allen, 1974), as well as the general ability to remember visual material (Milner and Taylor, 1972) and perception in the left half of our visual fields. In right hemisphere injuries, an individual may completely ignore the left half of a picture or a line of reading, a phenomenon labeled inattention or unilateral spatial neglect (Frantz, 1950; Gainotti and Tiacci, 1971).

The right hemisphere processes musical sounds, including pitch and rhythm (McFie, 1970), and may play a role in the rhythm and pitch of speech as well (Luria, 1966, 1973). Clients with right hemisphere injuries may show no musical skills at all, including an inability to determine rhythms and a deficit that resembles tone deafness.

The right hemisphere is not completely nonverbal but rather possesses some basic verbal abilities. Its receptive (understanding) skills are stronger than its ability to express itself (Gazzaniga and Sperry, 1967; Gott, 1973). The right hemisphere can understand some speech but cannot respond verbally.

Although the right hemisphere controls impulses to the left side of the body, the left side is also under control of the left hemisphere. This aids bilateral coordination of the actions of the right and left arms and legs.

LEFT HEMISPHERE. The primary function of the left hemisphere is the control of verbal behavior, including the ability to read, write, speak, and understand verbal material. The left hemisphere is directly responsible for the motor and sensory skills on the right side of the body and is also responsible for bilateral coordination of the left and right sides of the body. Thus, left hemisphere injuries generally produce more profound and general motor problems than right hemisphere injuries.

In addition to verbal skills, the left hemisphere is also involved in nonverbal spatial skills, although not to the same degree that the right hemisphere is involved (Benton, 1961; Hecaen, Ajuriaguerra, and Massonet, 1951; Luria, 1966, 1973; Osmon, Sweet, and Golden, in press). The left hemisphere contributes to our ability to cope with complex figures and spatial relationships (Brewer, 1969). Patients with left hemisphere injuries may draw an undistorted figure, but tend to simplify it. Patients with right hemisphere injuries will often distort the relationships of the parts within a complex drawing, but all the parts are often present (Golden, 1978).

Developmental Aspects of Brain Organization

Each area and skill within the brain develops at a different time in the development of a child. In general, functions of the first unit (attention, arousal) must develop before the second and third units can develop. Within the second and third units, basic skills must develop before more complex skills can be learned. Thus, basic sensory input must be established before a child can learn to process visual, tactile, and auditory input into meaningful units. Speech cannot develop until a child learns to integrate basic auditory input. Then the child must learn to pick out those sounds which have meaning. Skills such as reading cannot develop until these basic auditory and basic visual skills have developed.

Chronologically, those areas of the brain responsible for reading may not fully be developed physiologically until a child is seven. As a result, a significant number of first grade children are unable to learn to read, because the brain is not sufficiently developed.

In the third unit, basic motor control of individual limbs and of the tongue and mouth must be learned before more complex coordinated behavior is possible. An integration must be made between visual input and motor movements, which accompanies the beginning of planned behaviors. Higher cognitive skills, such as judgment, must await the maturation of the brain's prefrontal areas (located above the eyes), which may not be fully developed until seven or eight years of age.

The development of higher areas of the brain can be affected by the development of lower, more basic areas. Thus, injuries to the more basic areas can affect the development of the higher areas even if the higher areas are physiologically intact. This is an important factor in examining the brain injured child.

Summary

A modern approach to the organization of behavior in the brain was examined in this chapter. The theories of J. Hughlings Jackson and A.R. Luria were examined, emphasizing how these theories can account for the observations made by individuals in favor of a localization or an equipotential approach. The effects of losses in specific brain areas were discussed along with the concept of functional systems. Functional systems represent series of brain areas which operate in concert to produce a given behavior. The major units of the brain were discussed. The first unit is responsible for attention and arousal. The second unit involves sensory input and integration. The third unit is responsible for judgment, evaluation, and motor behavior. Differences in the cerebral hemispheres, involving the second and third units, were explained: the right hemisphere is primarily nonverbal, while the left hemisphere is verbal. Finally, the developmental implications of brain organization were briefly considered.

Chapter 6

THE FIRST UNIT:
AROUSAL AND EMOTION

THE FIRST MAJOR UNIT of the brain represents the most basic areas in the brain, consisting of the structures known collectively as the brain stem and the limbic system. In addition to their roles in arousal and emotion, these structures are also involved in the pathways which link the second and third units with the sensory organs and muscles of the body. Injuries to many of these structures may result in death or serious impairment. In addition, injuries to these structures caused by accidents generally involve many other areas of the brain as well. As a result, it has been difficult to study these areas directly in man. Most research has been done on animals, with theories of their roles in humans based on extrapolation and observations made by clinical observers.

The Reticular Activating System

The Reticular Activating System (RAS) makes up a major part of the first unit. The reticular activating system is made up of many groups of nerve cells which are dispersed throughout the brain stem and other structures of the brain. These nerve cells form a net which is directly involved in the arousal level of the human brain. The role of the RAS has been described by various authors as that of nonspecific (general) arousal (Papez, 1956), activation (Gastaut, 1958), and the induction of consciousness (Masland, 1958). The RAS is also involved in going to sleep, waking, and in remaining alert during the day (Chusid, 1970).

The RAS is closely related to the overall tone of the body. The higher the arousal levels induced by the RAS, the stronger a person's reactions to incoming stimuli. However, the unit can be selective about the type of stimuli to which it reacts. Consequently, activation can exist for a certain type of stimuli, e.g. a baby's cry, but not another, e.g. a plane going overhead every five minutes.

Three primary sources are responsible for activation by the RAS. The first is the metabolic processes of one's own body. Thus, arousal may be caused by the physiological need of the body to eat or drink. The second source of activation is stimuli from the outside world. An individual needs a certain level of sensory stimulation during waking hours. Outside events provide this stimulation to the system. Without these stimuli, the person may engage in self-stimulation, ranging from hallucinations to self-destructive behavior. It has been suggested that hyperactivity in some children is induced by this phenomenon. The child, under-stimulated because of a high need for stimulation or some injury that prevents a normal level of stimulation, must engage in constant activity to achieve a proper level of stimulation in the RAS. The third source of arousal comes from the third major unit of the brain and will be discussed in Chapter 8.

Emotional Reaction: The Limbic System

Extensive research has been conducted on the various components of the highly interconnected limbic system. The major components of the system include the hypothalamus, the amygdala, the septal area, and the hippocampus.

The hypothalamus has been associated with the regulation of horomone levels affecting such functions as digestion, sexual arousal, and circulation (Papez, 1958). It has also been associated with hunger, thirst, and day-to-day rhythms of the body (Neff and Goldberg, 1960; Symonds, 1966). The hypothalamus also appears to be closely connected with the feelings of pleasure and pain (Isaacson, 1974).

The amygdala appears to be related to automatic functions of the body, e.g. heart rate and respiration. Lesions of the amygdala can produce overeating in animals, and vicious attacks on food by humans under some conditions (Pribram and Bagshaw, 1953).

This food eating binge is often accompanied by enhancement of pleasurable events in general (Fonberg, 1973). Fonberg also reports that stimulation in another part of the amygdala may cause complete loss of eating behavior along with a loss of emotional reactivity. Dogs with amygdaloid lesions were described as either fearful and sad or happy and affectionate, depending on the location of the lesion.

The septal area is also involved in emotionality. After septal surgery, rats may appear to show rage reactions and be very emotionally reactive, although this reaction disappears in two to four weeks (Brady and Nauta, 1955). However, these symptoms have not been found in monkeys, although other animals may show increased sensitivity to stimuli (Isaacson, 1974). Generally, septal lesions change social behavior in animals, with some reports suggesting better social skills while others report less effective interaction (Isaacson, 1974). In novel situations, septal animals show an increase in activity, but quickly adapt to the situation and then show normal activity levels.

Of most interest in the study of learning disabilities is the behavior of animals with damage to the hippocampus. Isaacson (1974) and Isaacson and Kimble (1972) suggested that the behavior of animals with hippocampal lesions was similar to that of normal individuals who easily become frustrated. They found that animals with hippocampal lesions became very agitated and developed incorrect behaviors when faced with a situation in which rewards did not come with the regularity which the animal expected. Under these conditions, the animal engages in perseverative behavior, repeating sequences of behavior which did not lead to the goal the animal sought, even in instances when the animal "knew" the correct response. During this period the perseverative behavior consisted of long strings of inappropriate behavior during which the animal could be viewed as hyperactive. However, the main problem for the animals was not necessarily a higher level of activity but a higher level of inappropriate activity. This increase in inappropriate activity is one of the characteristics of the true hyperactive child. Nonneman and Isaacson (1973) also reported that the younger the animal was when the injury was suffered, the more likely it was to develop these problems. The authors also found extensive individual differences in the degree of symptoms, hypothesized to relate to an animal's inherent level of reaction to frustration.

In a similar manner, hyperactive children generally show very poor reactions to frustrating situations. They learn much better in situations where rewards are regular and expected. Like the results seen in many hippocampal lesioned animals, the hyperactivity tends to be constant and permanent.

Memory Problems in Hippocampal Injuries

The hippocampus is located in the "underside" of the temporal lobe in man. In a significant number of cases, surgical intervention was undertaken in individuals with "temporal lobe epilepsy" which involved the removal of much of the temporal lobe including the hippocampus. The purpose of these operations was to prevent the continuance of seizure activity which was resistant to all other forms of control. As a result, a population of adult humans was created which allowed the study of the effects of a lost hippocampus.

The most prominent effects in these injuries was the loss of memory skills. After injury to both hippocampi (one within each hemisphere of the brain), the subjects lost the ability to acquire new long-term memories. Thus, while the individual could remember events which happened previous to the injury, the subject could not remember what had happened to him or her the day before the interview. The subject still possessed short-term memory; they could memorize the sequence 2-4-6 if that was asked. However, if the person then talked about something else for a few minutes, he/she could not repeat the sequence of even a simple set of numbers (Penfield and Mathieson, 1974; Penfield and Milner, 1958; Scoville and Milner, 1957). The effects were not as dramatic if only one hippocampus were involved. A lesion or injury on the left side might produce some impairment of verbal memory (Russell and Espir, 1961), while lesions on the right side may lead to some impairment of nonverbal learning such as maze running (Corkin, 1965; Milner, 1965).

Lesions of Related Structures

Lesions of various structures in and around the first unit will cause other significant impairments as well, although these functions may not be directly related to the role of the first unit. However, they are important in day-to-day learning and in understanding the child with injuries in those areas.

CORPUS CALLOSUM. The corpus callosum permits communication and exchange of information between the right and left hemispheres. In adults, cutting the corpus callosum has little obvious effect because most stimuli in our environment are available, through the sensory organs, to both right and left hemispheres. However, special testing procedures do indicate a special role for the corpus callosum (Gazzaniga, 1966; Geschwind, 1965; Myers, 1959; Zaidel and Sperry, 1973). If the corpus callosum is cut and information is presented to one hemisphere using special techniques, that hemisphere will work independently of the other. For example, the right hemisphere could determine the answer to a nonverbal problem (for example, what object is formed by integrating a set of puzzle parts) but would be unable to verbally say the answer because it could not communicate with the left (verbal) hemisphere.

In cases of children where the corpus callosum fails to develop, the results are much more serious. Children born without a corpus callosum may often be mentally retarded (Loeser and Alvord, 1968) or, at least, show significant learning problems. In many cases, it is not clear whether the retardation is due to the loss of the corpus callosum or other deficits the children may have.

CEREBELLUM. The cerebellum is heavily involved in the basic processes necessary for general motor behavior. The cerebellum aids in keeping an individual oriented in space, and in keeping the body upright without conscious attempts to resist gravity. The cerebellum also monitors the background tone of voluntary movements started by the third brain unit (Chapter 8). Lesions in the cerebellum, depending on the location and extent, may cause a variety of disorders including tremors, jerky movements, flaccid muscles, inability to retain balance, disturbances of walking, and disturbances of eye movements (Chusid, 1970). No cognitive impairments accompany cerebellar damage. Children with lesions of the cerebellum and other parts of the motor system are usually given the diagnosis cerebral palsy. Such children may show no cognitive damage in addition to the motor problems but may be frequently misdiagnosed as retarded or learning disabled.

THALAMUS. The thalamus serves as the major pathway for sensory and motor impulses to and from the cerebral hemispheres. The right half of the thalamus relays information to the right hemisphere, while the left half relays information to the left hemisphere. Impairment of the thalamus may result in interruption of sensory information to one or both hemispheres, resulting in symptoms similar to a disorder of the second brain unit (Chapter 7), or may interfere with motor impulses to the muscles, resulting in symptoms resembling an injury of the third brain unit (Chapter 8).

Integrating the Functional Units

There is a tendency for many researchers investigating learning disabilities and brain injured children in general to concentrate on the cognitive functions of the second and third brain units rather than the functions of the first unit. However, as this survey has shown, lesions in the various parts of the first unit can cause many of the symptomatic problems associated with learning disabilities. Differential diagnosis of first unit or second or third unit deficits is important because the proper diagnosis in this case leads to radically different treatments. For example, lesions of the first unit respond much more effectively to treatment by medication than lesions to the second unit, even when the observable symptoms are the same. On the other hand, second unit symptoms will respond much faster and more favorably to behavior modification and educational programs than will first unit disorders.

Finally, it must be recognized that neither the second or third units could operate without the input and integration of the first unit. Although the reactions of the first unit can often be described as primitive and emotional, its role in determining higher cognitive behaviors is a major one which cannot be ignored.

Summary

The present chapter investigated the functions of the first major unit of the brain and closely related structures. Arousal, emotional reactivity, emotionality, and basic functions of the body were seen as major tasks of the first unit. A close approximation between hyperactivity and hippocampal lesions was pointed out, the effects of lesions in the cerebellum on motor behavior were detailed, and the role of the thalamus and the corpus callosum in data transmission between the cerebral hemispheres was discussed. Finally, the importance of the differential diagnosis of first unit disorders was emphasized.

Chapter 7

THE SECOND UNIT:
INPUT AND INTEGRATION

THE SECOND UNIT is responsible for receiving the major inputs from the outside world and integrating this information so that it can be used in a meaningful manner. Since knowledge of the outside world—the stimuli that determine what needs to be done and whether we are doing it—is indispensable to making accurate decisions, disorders of the second unit are commonly associated with mental retardation in more severe cases and learning disabilities in less severe injuries.

The functions of the second unit can be summarized as basic auditory, visual, and tactile reception and the analysis and integration of the inputs from different senses. The second unit deals with both verbal input (primarily in the left hemisphere) and nonverbal input (primarily in the right hemisphere). The unit has no direct connections to the outside world, but receives information from lower neural structures, which are connected to the sense organs, and forwards the integrated information to the third unit, which is responsible for ultimate motor input.

Auditory Functions

Information is relayed from the ears to the auditory nerve, which in turn conveys neural impulses through a series of connections to the temporal lobe areas in the right and left hemispheres (see page 41). The information received from the right ear primarily goes to the temporal lobe area of the left hemisphere; the information received at the left ear travels primarily to the temporal lobe area of the right hemisphere. Auditory information is received in a small area of each temporal lobe, called the primary reception area.

LEFT HEMISPHERE. The information which is received by the reception area is not organized. It is simply the neurally coded sequence of the sounds impinging on the ears. In the left hemisphere, these sounds are broken down into phonemes, the basic units of speech, by the secondary auditory areas which lie adjacent to the primary receptive area. These sounds are analyzed sequentially, in the order they are received. The ways in which the sounds are analyzed are the result of learning; that is, the process of phonemic analysis is not automatic but the result of teaching and sensitizing a child to certain sounds.

The secondary auditory area is also involved in verbal auditory memory. If sounds are to be perceived accurately as words and sentences, we must retain the sequence the sounds are heard. Finally, the auditory area is also involved in the analysis of the rhythm and pitch of speech, attributes which often determine subleties of meanings in verbal communication. However, more of the analysis of pitch and rhythm is done in the right hemisphere auditory areas (see below).

Injury to the primary receptive area on the left side may result in word deafness, which makes it impossible for the subject to understand speech, especially when subtle distinctions must be made in the sounds of letters, such as *d* and *t* (Neff and Goldberg, 1960; Zurif and Ramier, 1972). If this injury occurs after a child has learned to read and write, it will not interfere with those skills. However, if such an injury occurs before reading and writing are learned, it will make nearly impossible learning normal reading and writing. If the injury involves the primary receptive area in both hemispheres, the condition is equivalent to being deaf. Early injury to the primary receptive area of the left hemisphere can be among the most difficult to remediate.

Injury to the secondary auditory area of the left hemisphere may cause an inability to understand spoken speech. The effects of such injuries are often widespread, as the secondary area is responsible for the phonemic analysis necessary for reading, writing, and speaking. Consequently, lesions to the secondary area at any age can disrupt the full range of receptive and expressive verbal skills. The speech of such patients, if once normal, may disintegrate into only automatic phrases such as "you know" (Luria, 1963). The patient may show serious problems in analyzing rhythmic patterns as well (Lackner and Teuber, 1973). In milder forms of injuries to the secondary area, the patient may be able to speak, read, and write but confuses words with similar sounds, such as *bit* and *pit*.

RIGHT HEMISPHERE. The right hemisphere temporal receptive area is more concerned with the analysis of pitch, rhythm, and tone than it is with the analysis of verbal phonemes. However, the right temporal lobe is capable of verbal analysis. This is an important consideration in children with early injuries to the primary or secondary auditory areas in the left hemisphere: under the correct conditions, the right hemisphere auditory areas will attempt to take over the function of the left auditory areas, thus saving some speech functions.

Unlike the left hemisphere auditory areas, the right hemisphere areas are also involved in the decoding of visual patterns, especially those which are unfamiliar (Meier and French, 1965). Thus any unusual pattern—whether auditory or visual—may be analyzed in the temporal lobe of the right hemisphere.

Injuries to the right auditory areas, then, will interfere with the analysis of rhythm, tone, pitch, and unfamiliar material. Often, there may be a complete loss of musical skills or an inability to develop such skills. While there will not be a loss in understanding simple, basic phonemes, loss of the rhythm of speech may occur. Analysis of sounds which are essentially without verbal meaning may then be disrupted.

Visual Functions

Information is relayed from the eyes to the occipital region of the cerebral hemispheres, located at the very back of the head (see illustration). The information from the left half of *both* eyes is transmitted to the right hemisphere, while the information from the right half of both eyes is transmitted to the left hemisphere. Information from the eyes is transmitted on a point by point basis, and it is the responsibility of the brain to interpret figures, shapes, and so on. The two images from the left and right eye which go to each hemisphere are fused together by the brain in order to produce depth perception, a function which develops from birth.

The reception of the visual input is in the primary receptive area of the occipital lobe. Injury to either receptive area causes a partial or complete loss of vision in the half of each eye which transmit information to that primary receptive area. Losses in the primary area are permanent. Damage to the primary areas in both hemispheres results in complete blindness.

LEFT HEMISPHERE. Loss of the primary area in the left hemisphere eliminates visual input to those areas of the left hemisphere which determine verbal interpretation; consequently such individuals are unable to read or monitor their own writing. If the primary area is intact, the information received is integrated in the secondary visual area, the area responsible for the analysis of visual input. On the left side, the secondary visual area is especially important for the analysis of written verbal material. If there is an injury to the left secondary visual areas, the individual will still be able to decipher visual material, such as letters, but will be unable to read them. Such individuals can reproduce what is written (copy the patterns) but cannot appreciate them as verbal symbols.

With less severe injuries, the person can appreciate the nature of both letters and objects, but only one at a time. Thus, shown the word "READ" the person could eventually determine that the letters, R, E, A, and D were present, but not the order of the letters sequentially. Only one letter could be seen at a time, a condition known as simultaneous agnosia. A child with this injury may be able to learn specific letters and their meaning but will not be able to read. The disorder may also affect motor movements of the eye (discussed in Chapter 8). The eye will tend to jump all over the visual field rather than following a pattern useful for examining a verbal text or the environment. Visual-motor coordination is especially difficult in these circumstances.

RIGHT HEMISPHERE. The right hemisphere visual areas are more concerned with the analysis of patterns, especially unfamiliar patterns, than are the left visual areas. The secondary areas play a greater role in object perception and in spatial relationships of objects.

Disorders may make a person unable to appreciate the spatial relationship of one object to another. Thus, the person will have trouble constructing drawings, jigsaw puzzles, engines, or anything else that requires a knowledge of spatial relationships. Although there may not be a loss in verbal skills, the patient may be unable to accurately follow a line of writing, skipping instead from one line to another. This often appears as a dyslexia, an inability to read.

Lesions of the right visual area will also cause a phenomenon called inattention, in which the individual ignores the left side of everything that is seen. Thus, the client will see only the right half of a word or sentence, the right half of a book, and so on. In severe forms, the person will ignore the left side of his or her body. Such individuals cannot dress themselves because of an inability to acknowledge their own left arm or leg.

Tactile Functions

Information from the tactile senses, which include both the ability to touch and feedback from the muscles and joints that tell us the location of our limbs, are relayed to the primary receptive areas in the parietal lobe (see illustration). The information from the left side of the body is transmitted to the right parietal lobe, while information from the right side of the body is transmitted to the left parietal lobe. The input from the body is arranged so that the impulses from the feet, legs, trunk, arms, hands, and face lie in order along the central sulcus (see illustration). The amount of area devoted to each area of the body depends on the importance of the area to tactile perception. Thus the hands and lips, where the sense of touch is very important, get very large areas in the receptive area while the back gets a relatively small area. Parts of the body with larger reception areas have more sensitivity and stimuli can be located on them more precisely. Consequently, the ability to localize where one is touched is much stronger on the hands and lips than on the back.

Lesions of the primary area interfere with tactile sensitivity in those areas. The larger the lesion, the greater the loss of sensitivity. If the loss is in the receptive area for the hands, the person will be unable to recognize objects by touch, a disorder known as astereognosis. Astereognosis can also result from other important lesions.

LEFT HEMISPHERE. The secondary areas of the parietal lobes integrate the information received from the reception areas. They are responsible for localizing where one is touched, how an object or a limb is moving, and recognizing objects by touch when no deficits exist in the primary areas. Most importantly, the left secondary areas are very important in speech and writing. The movements necessary for writing are stored in terms of the impulses fed back from the joints and muscles of the hand. If there is an injury here, the brain cannot properly direct writing skills and the person confuses letters which are written in similar ways. In the same way, the person confuses spoken sounds which are pronounced in similar ways. Many disorders of reading and writing which appear motor in nature are often the result of tactile problems, and this distinction is important in rehabilitation programs.

Disorders of the secondary parietal area of the left hemisphere will cause problems in locating one's limbs in space, especially on the right side but involving both sides to some degree. The person is unable to copy movements shown him/her without visual help. Secondary lesions also result in the apraxic disorders, in which a person with no motor problems is unable to perform complex motor acts. These deficits may be seen in the learning disabled, so-called clumsy child.

A major disorder of the secondary areas is finger agnosia, an inability to recognize by tactile stimulation alone which finger is touched. (Heimburger and Reitan, 1961). In general, this occurs in the hand opposite the site of the injury. However, sufficient damage to the left parietal lobe can cause these deficits in both hands.

RIGHT HEMISPHERE. The tactile problems seen in left hemisphere injuries are seen in right hemisphere injuries, with deficits occurring on the left side rather than the right side of the body. However, right hemisphere tactile injuries do not affect speech or bilateral coordination to the degree that left hemisphere injuries do.

Integration Functions

Although the functions of the basic sensory receptive and analysis areas are important, they do not form the major tasks of the second unit. Of far more importance is the role of the second unit in integrating the senses. The integration forms the basis for most abstract thought and the "higher intellectual functions" that differentiate man from other animals. As might be expected, man uses a much greater percentage of his brain for these integration processes than does any other animal.

TACTILE-VISUAL INTEGRATION. In the left hemisphere, the tactile-visual areas, which lie between the primary tactile and primary visual areas, are responsible for the ability to locate ourselves in space and our idea of the layout of our bodies (Sauguet, Benton, and Hecaen, 1971). The patient with a disorder of this area may be unable to locate his or her own fingers without visual help. The area is also important for tasks involving sequencing. Kinsbourne and Warrington (1964) have related deficits in this area to an inability to spell, while others have found that general spatial dysfunction may come with lesions in this area, especially when the right hemisphere is involved (Brain, 1941). Disorders on the left side may lead to oversimplifications of drawings, while right-sided injuries may result in distortion of drawings.

With left hemisphere injuries, an individual can lose the ability to associate an object with its use and the ability to manipulate arithmetic symbols. She/he may also exhibit great difficulty in understanding the meaning of spatial words such as "above" or "below" or "beside."

TACTILE-AUDITORY-VISUAL INTEGRATION. This area lies near the center of the second unit and is responsible for complex cross-modal integration. In the left hemisphere, this area plays a major role in all verbal processes. The area is necessary for such basic skills as the ability to name objects, to remember verbal material, or the ability to name colors. In the right hemisphere, this area is basic to determining the basic angle of lines, the spatial manipulation needed in arithmetic (carrying over from "ones" to "tens," keeping proper spacing within numbers), and the ability to classify or order nonverbal material.

VISUAL-AUDITORY. Visual-auditory integration forms a major step in the process of reading. Lesions in this area lead to an inability to match visual symbols to auditory phonemes when visual and auditory systems remain fully intact. Specific lesions in this area form the purest example of dyslexia, the inability to read, in the absence of any other intellectual symptoms. In most cases of diagnosed dyslexia, however, the causes are generally more diffuse than in this limited disorder.

Summary

The functions of the second unit were reviewed, including the location and processes of the primary and secondary auditory, visual, and tactile areas. In addition, the functions of the integration areas of the second unit were also discussed. An attempt was made to discuss some of the deficits characteristics of specific lesions in each of these areas.

Chapter 8

THE THIRD UNIT:
JUDGMENT AND MOTOR BEHAVIOR

THE THIRD UNIT is responsible for all voluntary motor activity and for the judgmental decisions made by the person concerning what to do or what not to do on a voluntary basis. As a result, the functional level of this unit determines closely the level of behavior exhibited by a child or adult as well as the content of that behavior. In turn, however, the third unit is highly dependent on the second and first units for the information necessary to make decisions and the overall arousal necessary for behavior. In addition, the function of the third unit is influenced by the emotional tone of the first unit.

Interactions Between the First and Third Units

The first and third units are highly interconnected by brain pathways which carry impulses in both directions. As a consequence, the emotional reactions of the first unit can interfere with the processing of information by the third unit. If arousal levels are too high, the third unit may be unable to selectively ignore information fed from the second (input) unit of the brain. This overwhelming stimulation can result in an inability to make decisions, as is seen in some psychiatric disorders, or in behavior which is largely random and unfocused, as is seen in the case of the hyperactive child. Such behavior reflects a basic frustration response at being unable to handle or select the relevant stimuli from all those which enter the brain.

In addition, too little arousal will make the third unit unable to act intelligently when relevant stimuli are presented. The lack of arousal will lead to a general unresponsiveness in which the

61

person fails to react to any outside stimuli unless they are both large and imposing. This can make the individual withdraw or, in some cases, force the individual to engage in self-stimulation, when most behavior occurs within an individualized fantasy world unavailable to others. In many cases of frontal lobotomy, where the connections between the first and third units have been severed surgically, the patient gradually slips over time into a lethargy where he or she initiates less and less behavior.

The emotional reactivity of the first unit also plays an important role in third unit activity. If a given input is highly emotionally tinged, the third unit may be unable to consider any other source of information, leading to incorrect behavior. Similarly, stimuli accompanied by strong negative emotions can result in immobility and inability to think or basic avoidance behavior with little regard to the consequences. In less drastic cases, the emotional content of a stimuli as determined by the first unit can exaggerate or decrease the importance of an otherwise objective observation.

Properly taught, the third unit can control the reactions of the first unit. Thus, emotional behavior or unwanted high levels of arousal can be dampened by the actions of the third unit. The third unit can influence arousal or emotionality in any direction given the proper environment. Indeed, this relationship may explain why arousal problems, caused by injury to the first unit, can eventually be brought under voluntary control by behavior modification techniques properly applied.

RELATION OF THE SECOND AND THIRD UNITS. The second unit provides the third unit with all of its objective information about current activities in the outside world. Since the third unit is in charge of motor behavior, it requires constant feedback from the second unit to obtain information on the current state of behavior. For example, if one wishes to take a step, it is necessary to know which leg is currently in the air or on the ground. Lack of proper second-unit feedback is similar to walking through a dark, unfamiliar room.

Unfortunately, then, when the second unit malfunctions so does the third unit. If the second unit reports that our arms are in an upraised position when they are actually at our side, any motor movement will look clumsy and awkward, despite the fact that motor control is intact, a condition known as ataxia. Visual functions are highly dependent on feedback from the visual areas giving instructions on where to look and where one is currently looking. Without this feedback, the brain attempts to fixate upon something without knowing where it is starting from and without knowing when it achieves its goal.

Operation of the Third Unit

MOTOR AREAS. The motor areas lie along the posterior (back) end of the third unit, along the receptive tactile area. The motor area is designed so that the motor area for a particular part of the body lies adjacent to the tactile area for that part of the body (see Chapter 7). In addition to their close physical proximity, the two areas are interconnected by numerous pathways which provide for quick and easy interchange of information. Also, about 20 percent of the motor area cells consist of tactile receptive cells, while 20 percent of the tactile receptive area consists of motor output cells, further emphasizing the interrelated nature of tactile input and motor output. In fact, this interrelationship is so strong that many scientists prefer to think of the area as a "sensorimotor" area rather than consider them as separate motor and sensory areas.

The motor area is responsible for sending impulses which eventually direct the voluntary muscles of the body to perform. Generally, all behavior which is consciously directed originates from these motor cells. This behavior is further aided by the actions of the entire motor system which lies between these cells and the muscles, correcting for balance or the effects of gravity, forces we do not consciously consider.

In the newborn child, movements must be directed one by one. However, as we learn greater control and greater complexity of behavior, we see development of the premotor areas. Unlike the motor cells, which direct individual parts of the body in specific actions, the premotor areas organize sequences of behavior. The actions of the premotor area free us from having to consider the fine details of each sequence, such as writing our own name. Imagine how difficult writing would be if we repeatedly had to go through the laborious steps we followed in first learning to write. The difficulty is similar to that of the child whose injured premotor area is unable to learn such tasks as automatic sequences.

Injury to the primary motor areas results in paralysis of voluntary movement of the opposite side of the body. The destruction of the left motor area will lead to voluntary paralysis of the right arm and leg. In addition, the left motor area is intimately concerned with speech functions. Thus, impairment of the area will inhibit or eliminate all motor speech even in the absence of any intellectual deficits. Injury to the premotor areas does not result in paralysis but in an inability to carry out sequences of behavior. Lesions will lead to jerky, uncoordinated movements rather than smooth, purposeful movement of the limbs. Premotor lesions may also cause perseveration in which a response, once begun, is not stopped, as the premotor area cannot switch to a new behavior or stop the old one. One form of stuttering is a common example of this disorder.

PREFRONTAL AREAS. The prefrontal areas, the most forward parts of the third unit, represent the newest part of man's brain and the last area to fully develop in a child. This area is responsible for planning, structuring, and evaluating voluntary behavior. Severe destruction can lead to complete disintegration of behavior or the loss of the ability to develop any purposeful behavior (Elithorn, Piercy, and Crooskey, 1952). The patient may be echolalic, just repeating what is heard; may show strong perseverative behavior; or be inflexible, mute, and nonreactive to environmental cues (Luria, 1966). In many ways, this severe form of frontal lobe destruction is similar to the behavior of severely autistic children. In less severe lesions, the patient is able to follow simple commands but is unable to do activities requiring changes in activities or adapt to successively changing environments. Patients with frontal lobe disorders may have difficulty paying attention. They are often distracted by small noises or events that others are able to ignore easily (Luria, 1966). As a result, the patient's performance may actually appear to be much worse than the patient is capable of showing due to the normal distractions of everyday life. These patients are also very inflexible, finding it difficult to change activities or do things in a different way (Drewe, 1974; Malmo, 1974; Milner, 1963). Although these descriptions are drawn from cases with adults injured in the prefrontal areas, it is interesting how closely their behavior parallels that of some hyperactive children.

The deficits discussed above are associated with injury to the upper surface of the frontal lobes. When injuries occur to the lower surface, above the eyes, the results are not the same. The lower areas are associated with the connections between the third and first major units of the brain. Injuries to these areas may produce a change in the individual's level of arousal, resulting in the patient's becoming either apathetic and withdrawn or hyperactive (Luria, 1973). Emotional changes may be seen as well, with the patient losing control of inhibitions (Kramer, 1955; Luria, 1966, Sanides, 1964).

LEFT FRONTAL LOBE. Lesions of the motor area of the left frontal lobe in the third functional unit result in an inability to control speech, causing spoken speech to be garbled or impossible. Lesions of certain parts of the motor areas can fully destroy the inability to voluntarily utter speech sounds. Sometimes, the individual will be left with the ability to speak single sounds but will not be able to put them together to form words. Luria (1966) has suggested that the ability to think is also dependent on these areas of the brain. Consequently, loss of speech may be accompanied by an inability to form thinking patterns of any complexity. However, not all spoken speech losses result from injury to these areas: injuries to the muscles involved in speaking, to the pathways from the frontal lobes to the muscles, and certain areas of the first and second units may also result in speech loss without affecting the ability to think.

Lesions of the left frontal lobe may also lead to problems with word fluency (Benton, 1968; Milner, 1964; Ramier and Hecaen, 1970). The behavioral role of speech may be lost in some patients (Luria, 1966). These patients will state (truthfully) that they will do something, but never initiate the behavior. They may remember what they are told to do but not be able to do it, especially if they are required to do something complex or first make a decision (Luria, Pribram, and Homoskaya, 1964). The patient may also fail to determine adequately what is happening in the outside world and base decisions on impulses rather than an assessment of the best course of action (Luria, 1966).

RIGHT FRONTAL LOBES. Motor problems associated with right frontal disorders are similar to those described above, except they are generally less severe, primarily involve the left side of the body, and do not involve speech. Although speech is intact, the patient may lose the ability to sing a song (Botez and Wertheim, 1959). Patients may also have trouble with tasks involving complex sequencing (such as repeating a list of numbers backwards rather than in the way they were given) or three-dimensional spatial skills. However, especially with small lesions, disorders of the right frontal lobe can exist without any apparent problems.

Summary

The present chapter examined the role of the third unit, which is responsible for judgment and motor behavior. It was emphasized that the third unit is highly dependent on both the first and second units in order to function, and that it cannot develop without the input from these units. The role of the unit in motor behavior and planning and the effects of lesions in various areas of the unit were discussed. It was noted that the behavior of adults injured in these areas are highly similar to that of the hyperactive or clumsy child.

Chapter 9

THE EFFECTS OF BRAIN INJURIES IN CHILDREN

T HE PREVIOUS four chapters of this section have established the close relationship between area of injury and the symptoms shown by individuals with brain injury. Although most of this knowledge has been determined from the behavior of adults with brain injury, the evidence suggests that much of it applies to children as well. However, there are additional factors besides area of injury that must be considered to fully understand the effects of a brain injury in children.

Injuries Occurring Early in Life

Injuries occurring early in a child's life, before the child learns to speak, have different affects in a child than injuries which occur later in life. Depending on the extent and area of the injury, these injuries may be much more or much less disabling than adult injuries. Several important factors act to determine the outcome.

DIFFUSE INJURIES. Diffuse injuries are those which involve the entire brain. The term implies that little of the brain is left fully intact. These injuries produce the most severe effects of any type of brain injury. When a child receives an injury early in life, usually at or prior to birth, there has been no chance for the child to develop a set of skills which can be used to aid recovery. In addition, no intact areas of the brain exist to learn new skills at a normal level to help the child overcome the effects of the brain injury. As a result, the child typically shows poor skills in many areas. The child may be observed to show early motor and sensory deficits, show a delay in speech acquisition, and be unable to work with puzzles or simple toys. Such children are often given the diagnosis of mental retardation.

MASSIVE INJURIES IN ONE HEMISPHERE. Research in this area has concentrated on the behavior of children who have received hemispherectomies, complete removal of one cerebral hemisphere, usually for treatment of an uncontrollable epileptic condition. The research has indicated that the removal of the language dominant hemisphere (the left hemisphere in most children) results in significantly less speech impairment than the same operation in adults (Annett, 1973; Basser, 1962; Bruell and Albee, 1962; Geschwind, 1972; Hebb, 1942; Lansdell, 1969; Milner, 1974; Smith, 1975, 1976). These studies have clearly demonstrated that under the correct conditions one side of the brain can take over the functions of the other side.

However, this is at some cost to the child. The child rarely achieves normal intelligence performance, averaging a verbal IQ of 80 (100 is average) which places the child in the low "dull normal" range. In addition to a low verbal IQ, representing the inability of the spatial hemisphere to take over all speech functions, the child usually shows a low performance/spatial IQ which also averages about 80. It appears as if the price that is paid for the right hemipshere to assume the tasks of the verbal left hemisphere is the "sacrifice" of spatial skills which would otherwise have been normal. However, because of the importance of verbal skills, this exchange is clearly in the child's favor. There are cases of hemispherectomies in which this loss of IQ does not occur. For example, Smith (1976) reported a case of a child with a hemispherectomy who had an IQ over 120, just short of the range designated for the highest 2.5 percent of the population.

Several important factors determine occurrence of the phenomenon discussed above. First, the injury must be massive enough to involve substantial portions of what we have designated as the second brain unit (Chapter 2). Injuries to the first or third units do not appear to trigger this takeover mechanism if the second unit is intact.

A second important factor is the age at which the injury occurs. Research has demonstrated that dominance (the control by one hemisphere of verbal functions) appears even before a child is born. Connolly (1950) found that the temporal lobe, a major part of the auditory-verbal functioning areas, was larger in the left hemisphere than it was in the right hemisphere. This may enable the left hemisphere to establish verbal functions. Subsequent reports have consistently reported the same results (Geschwind, 1974). Wada, Clark, and Hamm (1975) found that the extra growth of the verbal areas was present as early as ten weeks before birth. After birth, the left hemisphere steadily becomes increasingly specialized in verbal functions while the right hemisphere becomes expert in spatial problems. The longer this relationship remains, the lower the likelihood that a child will be able to transfer functions from a newly injured left hemisphere to the right hemisphere. Especially after the child begins to talk (while possessing an intact left hemisphere), the likelihood of a substantial takeover becomes much less.

While most children are left hemisphere dominant for speech, about 8 to 10 percent of the population is right hemisphere dominant. In such children, verbal skills are developed in the right hemisphere while spatial skills develop in the left hemisphere. Thus, the reverse injury process must occur to these children. These children are usually from families where there is a history of left-handedness.

Left-handed individuals are often found to be mixed dominant. For some reason, either as a result of an injury or because of some inherited trait, these children develop speech representation in both hemispheres rather than one. As a result, these children can more easily have one hemisphere take over for the other when there is an injury. Thus, mixed dominant children and adults generally recover more quickly and more completely from brain injury than do individuals where one hemisphere is dominant. However, these individuals generally have more trouble learning complex verbal skills such as reading and writing even without a brain injury. This is related to the complexity of coordinating verbal skills in both hemispheres equally, rather than letting one "lead the way."

SMALL INJURIES. Unlike the larger injuries, small injuries do not cause a takeover by the intact hemisphere. These injuries do not seem to influence the brain's takeover mechanism, an unfortunate situation since these injuries would be more aided by takeover because of their limited effects. As a result, children with small injuries have an injury which prevents functional systems from developing as they normally would develop. This results in highly limited, specific disabilities, or what today we would call a specific learning disability. Because the rest of the brain remains intact, these disabilities are among the easiest to remediate. However, the earlier the injury is found and treatment begins, the more likely the chances for success (see Section IV). It is also important that the correct specific deficit be treated. It is not enough to know that there is a reading problem nor enough to know there is an auditory or visual problem. Depending on the location of the injury, almost any deficit can occur in these injuries.

Later Injuries

The later an injury occurs in a child who has shown otherwise normal development, the more the injury resembles that of the adult. As was the case with early injuries, however, we must discriminate again between diffuse, large, and small injuries.

DIFFUSE INJURIES. Boll (1976) found that children with diffuse brain damage at the ages of five to seven showed fewer deficits than children with injuries at ages two to four. Children aged two to four were in turn more intact than children with earlier injuries. This holds for all diffuse injuries: the older the child when injured, the less severe the effects. Luria (1966) explains this by noting that the older the individual at the time of an injury, the greater the number of functional systems already available which can make up for the loss in the ability to learn new skills. In the younger child, there is no such bank of skills to rely upon.

MASSIVE, UNILATERAL INJURIES. Unlike diffuse injuries, massive, unilateral injuries are more severe in children older than two. Because the opposite hemisphere is much less likely to take over skills in the older child, combined with the child's lack of functional systems to make up for lost behavior, this causes these injuries to be very serious in their effects. As a child grows older than two years, the deficits become less pronounced, as the child develops more ways of coping with the lost skills both intellectually and emotionally.

LOCALIZED, SMALL LESIONS. The effects of localized, small lesions becomes less pronounced as a child gets older. Depending on the location of the lesion, it is possible for a known brain injury to have no observable effects as alternate functional systems take over the duties of the injured systems. In some cases, however, this is not possible, especially when highly basic skills are involved (primary output and secondary integration areas). These injuries need rehabilitation training based on their localization.

Localization in the Brain

As was noted earlier, the localization of verbal and spatial skills appear to begin on a physiological basis even before birth. However, such localization is not complete until the child is at least several years of age. Thus, the localization data given in the previous chapters do not apply precisely to all children (or adults) in terms of relating psychological abilities to the status of the brain.

However, the types of abilities and relationships between abilities do remain. In all individuals, there is an area involved in auditory-visual organization, even if it is not precisely where it was placed in Chapter 7. Thus, psychological test results can tell us which behaviors are intact or lost, and what this means in terms of the skills that each area of the brain represents. It is not necessary to relate this to a specific brain injury in each child; localization is a handy way of saying "this child's deficits are identical to the ones we would see if the child suffered an injury in area X of the brain." In turn, this allows us to predict what kind of remediation or other help would benefit the child most, by invoking our understanding of how the brain organizes behavior and discovering an alternative organization using intact psychological skills.

The Etiology and Definition of Learning Disabilities

In discussing the definition of brain-based learning disabilities, it was indicated that a child or adult must have a specific disability in brain processes which interferes with academic or personal behavior. From the preceding discussions on the activity of the brain and the effects of various types of brain injury, we can now relate this general information to specific etiologies.

As has been noted, diffuse brain injuries do not result in specific deficits but in general disorders involving most or all brain processes. These children often perform at a mentally retarded level and rarely show specific deficits in single areas that are more impaired than other areas. Consequently, these injuries cannot produce disorders which can qualify as learning disabilities.

Less extensive injuries—whether large or small—which are localized within a single hemisphere do produce single specific areas of deficits. These deficits depend upon the age at which the child was injured as well as the location and extent of the injury. However, all are characterized by the presence of impaired areas in a child able to perform at normal levels in other psychological skills.

This definition also includes the child with a mild diffuse injury who has a larger, more specific injury as well. In these children, the key question is whether they meet the criteria of "normal skills" in some intellectual areas, which in turn is dependent on the severity of the diffuse injury. Although learning disabilities definitions would not include the child with a more severe diffuse injury plus an additional localized injury, the brain dysfunction involved is basically the same except for severity.

The definition has practical advantages, since a focal deficit can be documented through psychological testing with an adequate examination. As stated above, the physiological correlates of such deficits may remain unconfirmed in a given case, but the psychological test results can still be identified by a properly trained investigator.

Another advantage of this definition is the recognition that although there are sets of symptoms associated with brain injury, these symptoms differ considerably from child to child. Despite this, however, the symptoms for a given child must conform to the patterns of symptoms associated with a given injury at a given age. This avoids the problem of overly specific definitions of brain injury, which treat all brain injured children as equivalent, as well as the error of considering everyone with deficits as brain injured because they have problems with learning.

Before addressing the question of assessment in the next chapter, the relationship between the above definition and the definition of cerebral palsy should be examined. Cerebral palsy is defined as a disorder arising from an early brain injury which causes motor deficits. These lesions may be diffuse but they may be localized as well. Thus, the cerebral palsy child may often be learning disabled, the only difference in many cases being the presence or absence of distinct motor problems in the cerebral palsy child. Thus, there is considerable overlap between these groups. Many children designated as cerebral palsied can often benefit from many of the assessment procedures and rehabilitation techniques discussed in the next two chapters as a result of this close association.

Summary

The chapter reviewed the effects of specific brain injuries in younger and older children. It was shown that the effects of diffuse, massive lateralized, and small injuries differed considerably depending upon the age at which the injury occurred. The phenomenon of takeover by one hemisphere was discussed, and its relationship to the idea of dominance were discussed. Finally, this information was integrated with the results from previous chapters to produce a working definition of the brain injured, learning disabled child.

Section III
ASSESSMENT

Chapter 10

EVALUATING LEARNING DISABILITIES

BEFORE EXAMINING the tests used to evaluate learning disabilities, it is necessary to specify the important issues in testing the learning disabled child and to discuss the characteristics of the ideal tests or test procedures. Most of the information necessary for implementing assessment procedures can be derived from the literature presented in the preceding nine chapters and from an evaluation of the practical limitations facing the assessor of learning disabilities.

The Role of the Medical Examination

As has been presented, many learning disabled children show soft neurological signs and a small percentage show hard neurological signs. Abnormal EEGs are also often seen in these children. As a result, it is imperative that any learning disabled child receive a thorough neurological examination, preferably from a specialist in the area of pediatric neurology. The importance of a specialist with proper training cannot be overemphasized. Pediatric neurology is a difficult area because of the changes necessary in giving and interpreting the neurological examination as a function of the child's age, and the physical difficulty of eliciting proper responses from young children.

It is rare for a learning disabled child to receive medical treatment. In most cases where equivocal signs are found, little or no treatment is indicated. In those cases where definite brain injury is indicated, it is usually an old brain injury which has recovered as much as can be expected. One major exception to this rule is the learning disabled child in which seizure disorders are found. These can often be treated medically, with subsequent improvement in both the child's medical status and learning skills.

Another exception is the child with current, ongoing brain injury or a brain disorder such as hydrocephalus (in which fluid-filled cavities within the brain become abnormally enlarged), tumors, or congenital arterial malformations (abnormalities in the vessels carrying blood within the brain). It should be emphasized that these conditions are quite rare, but it still remains quite important to rule these conditions out.

The final instance in which medical treatment is sometimes appropriate is the case of the hyperactive child. Although many such children do not need treatment with the various medications which have been proposed for treating hyperactivity, some clearly do. The conditions under which this is most effective are discussed in Chapter 17.

In addition to identifying the child in need of medical treatment, the neurological examination can be useful as one piece of evidence employed in determining the nature of the learning disability (if any) in the individual child. The results of the neurological examination, combined with the results of educational and psychological evaluations, are effective in answering questions necessary for understanding and determining the proper treatment for the child.

The Educational Examination

A comprehensive educational evaluation is necessary to determine the educational strengths and weaknesses of the individual child. This allows the examiners to identify the specific areas in which a child shows impairment, as well as the specific areas of academic strength a child may possess. The educational assessment permits determination of educational deficits which must be explained in any evaluation of the child's brain processes.

Results of the educational examination require careful consideration to give accurate portrayal of the child's abilities. First, a failure to do well on an educational test does not mean that a child is learning disabled. A failure to achieve, even in a child with a normal IQ, may be due to many reasons. A child may not wish to learn (a motivational problem); the child may be emotionally disturbed and unable to concentrate; a child may not have attended school, as in the case of a habitually truant student; or, if the child attended school, she/he may never have worked to learn the material. While some children in these categories may be learning disabled, it is unfair both to schools and children to classify all nonachieving children into the category learning disabled, as children in each of the different categories need help very much different from that offered the learning disabled child.

A second important focus in evaluating the learning disabled child is that a given educational deficit may not be caused by brain injury even in a brain injured child. Although it may often be assumed that if a child is brain injured, then all of the child's problems must be due to the brain injury, in actual practice, this is rarely the case. Often, brain injured children develop emotional problems as a result of the reactions they receive from other children, parents, teachers, and others, or as a result of their own frustration at being different from other children. Because of this, it is imperative that we understand the areas of a child's learning problems as completely as possible. Only with such information can we relate the result of the examination of a child's brain processes to the child's learning problems, so that we can understand which deficits are due to the brain injury and which are due to other problems.

The tests available for the educational examination of the child vary considerably depending on such factors as the school material used in a given setting, the techniques employed by teachers, and the grade level of the child. Individual techniques used by the experienced individual teacher may sometimes be better than complex instruments which bear little relationship to the teaching methods of a particular school. In any case, it is important that decisions be made on the basis of individually administered tests rather than a group test filled out by the child alone or in a larger group.

The Neuropsychological Examination

The purpose of the neuropsychological examination is to evaluate all of the abilities which represent the basic functions of the brain. The areas assessed include basic sensory (tactile, visual, and auditory) the motor functions, the functions of the sensory integrating areas, and the functions of the frontal lobes (planning, evaluating, flexibility). In addition, the child's behavior must be evaluated for evidence of hyperactivity or other movement disorders. Although it is not always practical to perform an examination covering every area completely because of time or manpower limitations, it is necessary to perform as complete an examination as possible, especially in problem areas.

Some would argue that a comprehensive examination is not necessary. These clinicians suggest that one need only concentrate in that area or areas that the child has academic or behavioral problems based on teachers' reports, parents' reports, or the educational or medical evaluation. Thus, what time is available can be used to concentrate on the important deficits. While this is a reasonable argument, it has several flaws. First, it assumes we know fully the likely nature of a child's problem. In practice, however, deficits in such skills as reading and writing may arise from lesions throughout the brain. Our ability to identify a particular deficit which may interfere with reading does not mean we have identified all deficits that interfere with reading. It is not rare for a brain injured child to have losses in several skills, each of which impairs performance of a given academic skill. Without a comprehensive evaluation, we may miss one or more of the problems involved in a particular loss, undermining our rehabilitation techniques because of an inadequately developed program. Secondly, the rehabilitation programs are often dependent on the state of the brain as a whole, not just one area (Section IV).

In designing a comprehensive examination, it is not necessary to restrict the examination to psychologists. Many parts of the examination can be completed by a variety of professionals from ophthalmology, speech pathology, occupational therapy, physical therapy, recreational therapy, and education. However, whether the examination is completed by a single individual or a team of experts, just as the brain is a single organ and no area of the brain can function by itself without the interaction of the remainder of the brain, the report from only one test or profession is unable to stand without the input from the remaining areas. Results from different tests and professionals must be integrated into a single report which points out the overall relationships of the test results and their implications for the function of the brain. The final results, no matter how many people collaborated in designing them, should consist of only one integrative report rather than single reports from each area. Although this is a difficult task, it is absolutely essential to the integrated understanding of the child.

Methods of Analyzing Test Results

In analyzing the test results from a large set of test scores gathered from a series of tests or from a group of professionals in different areas of evaluation, it is important to use analysis techniques specifically aimed at inferring the operation of the brain. These techniques are, in many cases, similar to those used in research to detect the presence of brain injury in children (Chapter 3).

LEFT VERSUS RIGHT MOTOR SKILLS. This technique involves comparing motor performance of the right hand to the left hand. In an individual who is right-handed, it is expected that the right hand will be 10 percent faster and stronger than the left hand. If an individual child differs considerably from this expectation, there is a strong suggestion of brain dysfunction. If there is a deficit in the right hand, the injury is in the left hemisphere; if the deficit is in the left hand, the injury is in the right hemisphere.

LEFT SENSORY VERSUS RIGHT SENSORY. In general, the left and right halves of the body should have the same sensitivity to touch, temperature, and movement; the right ear should be equal in hearing skills to the left ear; and sight should be equal in the right and left halves of each eye. Any deviation from these relationships suggests brain injury. In both motor and sensory comparisons, it is necessary to rule out peripheral injuries to the sense organs, bones, muscles, or skin that might cause impaired performance. It is also necessary to rule out injuries to the spine, which can result in symptoms which mimic brain injury.

VERBAL VERSUS NONVERBAL SKILLS. Although it is a simplification (see Section II), the left hemisphere controls verbal skills while the right hemisphere controls nonverbal skills. Thus, if verbal skills are significantly below nonverbal skills, or vice versa, this is also suggestive of brain injury. It is very important in these cases, however, not to use this method alone to determine brain injury, since many children without learning disabilities have impairment in specific skills, especially in verbal areas. For example, children with divergent cultural backgrounds may show "impairment" in English language skills.

PATTERN ANALYSIS. This technique represents the mainstay of the diagnosis of learning disabilities resulting from lesions of the brain. Pattern analysis asks whether the entire pattern of test results are consistent with a lesion in a given area of the brain at a given age. This technique is indispensable to localizing and verifying the existence of a localized lesion which could result in a learning disability. Only when the child conforms to a pattern representative of a given injury can we state that the child is likely to have suffered a brain injury (dysfunction) of some kind.

Pattern analysis requires that a child's test scores be consistent with each other before a diagnosis can be made. This avoids the situation in which a child is given a diagnosis of brain dysfunction merely because she/he has a given deficit, such as an inability to read. A pattern analysis would require the reading deficit to be accompanied by specific sensory, integrative, or motor deficits consistent with a specific lesion within the brain before a diagnosis of brain injury was made.

There has been extensive research on test score patterns associated with lesions in specific areas of the brain and occurring at specific ages. Since each area of injury produces a different pattern, it is necessary for an individual employing pattern analysis to have extensive background in the effects of injuries on brain functions, as different locations of injury can change test results. Thus, only with supervised training and applied experience with brain injured children or adults can one attain competence in this process. Readers interested in a general idea of test results found in different injuries may examine Golden (1978).

Age Problems

The diagnosis of the child presents a much more difficult task for the neuropsychologist than does the diagnosis of adult brain injury. One of the major factors in this difficulty is the role of the age of the child. Children change quickly in the kind of skills that we can expect them to do. A child whose performance would be normal at four years old may not be normal at five years old. However, all children who are four years old are not at the same developmental level. Some children may be developmentally advanced and be at the level of a child a year older, while another child may fall at the level of children a year younger. If we compare the fast-developing four year old to normal four year olds, we find that the child performs at a normal level in areas which are impaired relative to the child's other skills. However, if we compare a slow-developing four year old with a normal four year old, we find ourselves consistently classifying the child as "brain injured" or "impaired."

Thus, it is necessary to take developmental factors into account. The basic rule is to examine each child to determine if the assumption that the child is developmentally ahead or behind his current level makes the test data more consistent and understandable. If this is the case, then we can tentatively accept such a hypothesis and analyze the test scores and make interpretations on that basis. This approach is highly dependent on the use of multiple tests so that the pattern changes can be observed. If done with only one test, the technique always concludes that the child is simply developmentally different, whether or not that is the case. When this technique is employed, the set of assumptions that clarify the child's test scores most effectively and relate to the observed behavior of the child most closely are accepted as being most likely correct.

The Role of Dominance

As originally defined, the dominant hemisphere was thought to be the hemisphere which controlled verbal skills. Thus, in most individuals, the left hemisphere would be dominant because it controls verbal function. In some individuals (less than 10% of the population), this situation is reversed: the right hemisphere controls verbal skills.

In most individuals, the dominant hemisphere also controls

the dominant hand, eye, and foot. Thus, in individuals with a left hemisphere dominance for speech, we would expect the dominant hand, eye, and leg to be on the left side. In actual practice, this is not the case. In right-handed individuals, the left hemisphere is dominant 96 percent of the time while in left-handed individuals, the right hemisphere is dominant only 15 percent of the time (Milner, 1975). Thus, while normal right-handers follow the predicted pattern, normal left-handed individuals do not.

Considerable interest has been expressed in the phenomenon of mixed dominance. In this disorder, the side (right or left) of the dominant hand, leg, and eye do not agree. Mixed dominance of this type is almost nonexistent in normal right-handed individuals, while it is seen in 15 percent of the normal left-handed population. In individuals with early brain injury, however, 6 percent of the right-handed patients are mixed dominant while 19 percent of the left-handed patients are mixed dominant (Milner, 1975). Thus, there is a slight increase in mixed dominance in the brain injured population of about 5 percent.

A second type of mixed dominance occurs when the hemisphere controlling verbal skills is not the hemisphere controlling the dominant hand, eye, and foot. In normal right-handers, this occurs 4 percent of the time, while in normal left-handers we see it nearly 70 percent of the time (Milner, 1975). Milner found that among brain injured patients, this phenomenon occurs 13 percent of the time in right-handed patients and 30 percent of the time in left-handed patients. Thus, there is an increase in this phenomenon in brain injured right-handed patients but a decrease in brain injured left-handed individuals.

Some have postulated that in mixed dominant individuals verbal skills are not dominant in one hemisphere but represented in both. It has been theorized that this may cause problems in verbal skills leading to learning disabilities because of conflict between the hemispheres or the inefficiency of using two hemispheres for a single task. However, the figures on mixed dominance do not suggest a high enough incidence to blame most learning disabilities on this phenomenon, although some children may have learning disabilities arising out of this problem.

Dominance in children and adults can be assessed in a variety of ways. Generally, the dominant hand is the one used for writing and other basic tasks (nailing, opening doorknobs, etc.). A number of tests for hand, eye, and foot dominance have been developed and are in use (Crovitz and Zener, 1962; Oldfield, 1971). However, mixed dominance, especially in left-handers, may not reflect brain injury, nor does the absence of mixed dominance imply normality.

Summary

The chapter examined the primary issues in the assessment of learning disabilities. The role of the medical examination in ruling out serious medical disorders and contributing to the understanding of the patient was discussed, along with the role of the educational examination in pinpointing academic problems. It was emphasized that educational deficits alone do not define a learning disability. The need for a comprehensive evaluation of brain based skills was explained, showing how such an evaluation allows for a more complete understanding of a child's problem. The need to integrate the data from diverse tests and professions was pointed out as necessary to understand the child as a unique individual.

The primary methods of analyzing test results were discussed, with the emphasis on the role of pattern analysis in establishing the existence of learning disabilities. The problems of developmental changes in children were outlined. It was indicated that the developmental hypothesis must be considered in the case of each child. Finally, mixed dominance and its role in brain injury were discussed.

Chapter 11

THE INITIAL ASSESSMENT

ALTHOUGH a comprehensive examination is desirable in all learning disabled children with brain injury, it is neither feasible nor helpful to do such examinations on all children with school problems. As a result, it is necessary to establish initial screening procedures which estimate whether a child is likely to be brain injured. In children in which brain injury is a strong likelihood, the more extensive neuropsychological examination (Chapter 12) may be used as a follow-up to the screening procedures.

Assessing the Value of a Screening Procedure

Many tests have been developed as screening procedures for brain disorders causing learning disabilities. While the value of some tests have been extensively documented in the professional literature, others have little or no documentation of their effectiveness except for testimonials from professional or lay users. The reader must be very critical about the test that has little scientific documentation. Because of the difficulties in defining learning disabilities and brain injury in the first place, tests can be developed which *seem* to work and be useful when in fact they are no more effective than examining a child with no tests at all.

In tests investigated with scientific research, several questions must be asked. First, is the test *reliable?* An important aspect of this question asks whether the child would continue to get the same score in the test if given it twice. If the scores a child gets are not the same for two testings, it is difficult to see the usefulness of the test. On one day, the test may suggest there is a learning disability; on the next day, it may suggest there is no learning disability.

A second requirement is *standardization.* Standardization refers to the way a test is given: the instructions used, the procedure, the materials, the time given, and so on. Even if a test is effective in a research study, it must be given the same by everyone who uses it. If this is not done, then inaccurate results will be found. The test scores will not mean the same things as they are supposed to mean. For a test to be fully standardized, all individuals who use the test should give it in a nearly identical manner.

The third primary issue is *validity.* Does the test measure what it is supposed to measure? If a test claims to be related to brain damage, then the test must show that it can accurately diagnose brain damage and the conditions under which it can make such a diagnosis. Without this evidence, the claims of the test makers are meaningless. In many cases, tests are based upon theory rather than actual cases of brain damage. A theory of brain damage must be shown to work with specific cases of brain damage. In the case of learning disabilities and brain damage, the test needs to be able to identify the dysfunction related to learning disabilities.

Requirements of a Screening Battery

Usually a screening procedure must consist of more than one test, since we have seen that brain injury can cause a wide array of symptoms. The most ideal screening procedure will cover each major area (Verbal, nonverbal, auditory, tactile, visual, motor, planning, and flexibility) to some degree, while at the same time keep the procedure short enough to allow it to be given to many children. It is neither desirable nor useful to cover any single area in any great detail initially, as this can be done when it is decided that a more extensive examination would be productive.

There are many ways to complete the task suggested above, as there is no single set of procedures that make up an ideal screening battery. The choice of tests is often based on personal training and preferences. However, certain tests appear to be used more extensively and effectively than others for this purpose. The remainder of the chapter will briefly cover some of the most representative tests used as screening procedures.

Wechsler Intelligence Scale for Children

The Wechsler Intelligence Scale for Children (WISC) and its recent revision, the Wechsler Intelligence Scale for Children-Revised (WISC-R), is the most used test in the assessment of learning problems for children today. The test has several advantages over other procedures. First, it is the accepted measure of IQ in children aged six to fifteen. An overall intelligence estimate may be determined by the test, allowing for an examination of the child's general intellectual level. Second, the test is actually a test battery of twelve tests, each of which measures several verbal or nonverbal skills. The twelve tests in the battery can be compared to one another to yield a rough idea of whether or not there is likelihood of a brain injury. Third, the test has been shown by research to be highly sensitive to brain injury in children (Reitan, 1974; Boll, 1974). Finally, the test is extremely well standardized and has been repeatedly shown to be a very reliable and valid test (see Sattler, 1974, for an excellent review and introduction to the use of the WISC and other tests of intelligence in childhood).

THE SUBTESTS. As noted above, the WISC contains twelve subtests. Six of these subtests are verbal tests used to determine a verbal intelligence quotient, while the remaining six tests are performance tests used to determine a performance (nonverbal) intellectual quotient. The twelve tests together combine to yield a full-scale IQ (intelligence quotient). This is the figure most often referred to when discussing a child's IQ, although certain analyses for learning disabilities look closely at the relationship between the verbal, performance, and full scale IQ.

The verbal subtests are Information, Comprehension, Arithmetic, Similarities, Vocabulary, and Digit Span. *Information* is a measure of the facts we learn from normal experience with our environment. The test score may be related to the richness of the child's surroundings and the effectiveness of his or her school experience. The test requires long-term memory functions. *Comprehension* measures one's judgment or common sense. Individuals are faced with day-to-day situations or proverbs which must be explained. Scores on the test are related to social judgment, as well as the type of experience to which a child has been exposed. *Arithmetic* measures the ability to do simple arithmetic operations. Good performance requires basic mathematical skills, the ability to work from word problems to arithmetic problems, and the ability to concentrate and pay attention until an answer is reached.

Similarities measures an individual's ability to find relationships between pairs of words. Thus, it is a measure of abstraction and concept formation. *Vocabulary* measures a child's ability to define words which range from the very easy to the relatively difficult. The test measures not only familiarity with words but also the ability of the child to speak expressively and form verbal concepts. *Digit Span* is a test of memory in which the child is required to remember increasingly longer strings of numbers. In the first part of the test, the child must simply repeat the numbers given. In the second part of the test, the child must repeat the numbers backwards. The first section measures attention, concentration, and immediate memory. The second measures each of those skills as well as the ability to reverse the string of numbers into an alternate sequence.

The performance tests on the WISC include Picture Completion, Picture Arrangement, Block Design, Object Assembly, Coding, and Mazes. The *Picture Completion* subtest requires a child to look at a picture with a part missing and to identify the missing part. It is a test of the ability to recognize what are essential details in a given object and then to determine their presence or absence. The test also requires visual concentration and visual decoding skills. *Picture Arrangement* consists of cartoon stories which must be put into the proper order by a child. The test requires the child to interpret the visual pictures and arrange them into a story that makes social sense. Thus, it is a test of planning ability and the ability to consider alternative answers until the proper one is found.

Block Design requires the reproduction of a design visually presented using colored blocks. Thus the child must decode the printed design, breaking it down into its component pieces, which in turn must be reproduced using the blocks at hand. The test

is a good measure of spatial skills, although an impaired performance may also be due to the inability to reproduce the design
rather than the inability to break it down (Sattler, 1974). *Object
Assembly* consists of four jigsaw puzzles which must be completed
within a set time limit. The test requires visual perception,
visual integration, motor skills, and concentration. *Coding* is a
measure of visual-motor coordination and short-term memory.
The child must associate two sets of symbols with one another.
Since one set of symbols must be written below the second set,
there is a strong element of motor speed in this subtest. The
Mazes subtest consists of maze problems which the child must
complete. The test requires planning ability (finding the solution), motor skills (drawing in the solution), and the ability to
visually scan the entire problem.

As can be seen in the short description of the tests above, many
of the major components of basic brain skills are covered in the
Wechsler tests. None, however, are a pure measure of any skill;
all are complex combinations of different abilities. Thus, it is
difficult, if not impossible, to identify the exact nature of most
learning disabilities by the scores on the WISC; however, the test
is often sufficient to identify the presence of a disorder likely to
be related to brain activity.

Many authors have attempted to identify patterns of WISC
scores which suggest the presence of a learning disability or brain
dysfunction. One major emphasis has involved looking at the
difference in scores between the verbal and nonverbal tests (Reed,
1967; Rourke and Flewelling, 1971). These studies and many
others (Golden, 1978) have indicated that significant differences
in verbal and performance IQs may be related to injuries in one
hemisphere. For example, left hemisphere injuries may show up
in lower verbal scores while right hemisphere injuries may appear
in lower performance scores. Although this relationship does not
hold uniformly for each individual child, large differences suggest an area to be investigated in a given child.

Other authors have looked for patterns of individual test
scores. For example, several studies have found that learning disabled readers show low scores on Information, Arithmetic, and

Coding while they show relatively higher scores on Comprehension, Vocabulary, Object Assembly, Picture Completion, and Picture Arrangement (Lyle and Goyen, 1969). This pattern of test scores is consistent with an early, localized lesion in the second brain unit of the left hemisphere (Chapter 7). Low scores on Digit Span (auditory memory) have also been found in neurologically impaired learning disabled children (Ackerman, Peters, and Dykman, 1971). A pattern analysis approach to WISC scores involves comparing the child's tests to national averages as well as to the child's own average score, so that both the level of the child's performance compared to the performance of others and the relationship of one test to another for the individual child can be ascertained (Golden, 1978; Leton, 1972). These patterns can then be related to the neuropsychological organization of the brain suggested in Section II to determine whether a likelihood of brain injury exists. Readers interested in specific test score patterns are referred to Golden (1978).

Bender-Gestalt

The Bender-Gestalt has been used in numerous studies examining minimal brain dysfunction and other problems in young children (see Koppitz, 1963, 1975 for excellent reviews of the research and clinical applications of this test). The Bender involves administration of nine pictures which must be copied by a child. Thus, it is basically a measure of the child's ability to visually decode the picture and then motorly reproduce it. The inability to do this is called *construction dyspraxia*. The test also requires attention and concentration from the child. Impulsive children will also produce inadequate drawings.

Much of the research relating the Bender-Gestalt to brain damage has already been described in Chapter 3 and will not be repeated here. In summarizing that research, it was found that many children with signs of brain injury and also many normals show poor Bender performances. Thus, using the Bender one might find that 70 to 90 percent of the brain injured children show poor performance, but about 20 to 30 percent of the normal children would show poor performance as well. Half the children with emotional disturbances may show inadequate Benders.

Despite its limitations, the Bender is a useful measure of construction dyspraxia and visual motor skills. Used in conjunction with another test, such as the WISC, it can be very useful in the screening of potentially learning disabled, brain injured children.

Frostig Test

The Frostig Test was originally developed to aid in the diagnosis of neurologically handicapped, learning disabled children (Frostig, Lefever, and Whittlesey, 1961). The test consists of five subtests: Eye-motor Coordination, Figure Ground, Form Constancy, Position in Space, and Spatial Relations. Unfortunately, much research has found the Frostig to be unreliable in its subtest scores (Hammill, Collarusso, and Wiederholt, 1970). This means that each test does not reliably measure what it purports to measure. Black (1974) concluded that the Frostig's ability to predict performance in school was solely related to the test's overall correlation with intelligence. Olson and Johnson (1970) concluded that by the time a child was six, the Frostig was a poor predictor of school performance problems.

Overall, these results do not suggest any special advantage for the Frostig Test over the WISC as a screen for learning disabilities. It is especially clear that the Frostig is highly inadequate as a diagnostic instrument for learning disabilities when used alone. Hallahan and Cruickshank (1973) have concluded that the Frostig can be used only with great caution in the design of rehabilitation programs for learning disabled children.

Illinois Test of Psycholinguistic Abilities

The Illinois Test of Psycholinguistic Abilities (ITPA) is another test developed in an attempt to diagnose learning disabled children (Kirk, McCarthy, and Kirk, 1961, 1968). The test consists of nine subtests, each of which theoretically measures a separate skill. Specific disabilities on a given test suggest specific rehabilitation programs. The nine subtests are auditory decoding, visual decoding, auditory-visual association, visual-motor association, vocal encoding, motor encoding, auditory-vocal ability, auditory-vocal sequencing, and visual-motor sequencing. However, research has suggested that these are not independent skills as has been suggested by the authors. In addition, subtests tend to be unreliable when used alone for diagnosis (Burns and Watson, 1973; Waugh, 1975). Like the Frostig, the ITPA seems to be a general measure of verbal intelligence rather than a specific diagnostic test (Hallahan and Cruickshank, 1973).

Many of the same conclusions reached about the Frostig are appropriate for the ITPA. It cannot be used, as the authors claim, for specific rehabilitation programming but only as a general screen.

McCarthy Scales of Children's Abilities

The McCarthy Scales of Children's Abilities is a set of intellectual measures intended for children between the ages of 2.5 and 8.5. Although a relatively new test (McCarthy, 1972), it has been extensively validated and proven to be useful in the assessment of children with learning disabilities. In the most comprehensive source book on the McCarthy scales to date, Kaufman and Kaufman (1977) outline the advantages of the McCarthy scale in assessing learning disabled children. First, the test offers a wide variety of subtests measuring both verbal and nonverbal skills. The test offers a more detailed screening evaluation than most of the tests available for very young children. Second, research has suggested that the test may be sensitive to the presence of learning disabilities (DeBoer, Kaufman, and McCarthy, 1974; Kaufman and Kaufman, 1974). One deficit of the test is that it has not been extensively used with brain injured, learning disabled children, so we are not aware of its full potential or lack of potential in that area. Thus, although the test appears to measure a wide range of skills important in the screening examination, we cannot at this time fully assess its value. However, in children, especially those below the age of seven, it would appear to be an extremely useful and valuable device.

SUBTESTS. The McCarthy consists of eighteen subtests. These include Block Building, Puzzle Solving, Pictorial Memory, Word Knowledge, Number Questions, Tapping Sequence, Verbal

Memory, Right-Left Orientation, Leg Coordination, Arm Co-ordination, Draw-a-Design, Draw-a-Child, Numerical Memory, Verbal Fluency, Counting and Sorting, Opposite Analogies, and Conceptual Grouping. As can be inferred from the names of the subtests, many of the major skills involved in brain function are assessed briefly by the test. While one could not make a definitive diagnosis on the basis of the McCarthy, it would appear to offer a good potential as a screening test in young children.

Kaufman and Kaufman (1977) observe that the overall result of the McCarthy in learning disabled children is about 15 points less than the overall IQ the child would obtain on the WISC. It is not clear whether this represents a greater sensitivity to learning disabilities on the McCarthy or is a function of the different normative samples used for the McCarthy and the WISC. In any case, overall scores should not be important in the diagnosis of a brain-based learning disability. The pattern analysis of the subtests should yield considerably more useful information.

Summary

The present chapter covered the topic of initial screening procedures in the evaluation of possible learning disabled children. The four basic requirements for screening tests were reviewed: standardization, reliability, validity, and a covering to some degree of the major functions of the brain. However, the screening test need not be comprehensive in any one area. Major tests which are used for screening were reviewed, including the Wechsler Intelligence Scale for Children, the Bender-Gestalt, the Frostig, the Illinois Test of Psycholinguistic Ability, and the Mc-Carthy Scales of Children's Abilities. At present, a combination of the Bender (or a similar test) and the WISC appear to be most useful as a screening procedure in older children. The McCarthy tests appear promising, along with the Bender, as a test for children under seven.

Chapter 12

THE COMPREHENSIVE EXAMINATION

AFTER a child has been found to have a high likelihood of a learning disability due to a dysfunction of the brain, it is necessary to evaluate comprehensively the child's neuropsychological abilities. Although it is easy to require a comprehensive examination, there is difficulty in defining practically what such an examination includes. What one psychologist may consider comprehensive may not meet the definition another would use. In each case, then, it is necessary to evaluate the examination given a particular child to see if all the major areas covered by brain function (Section II) are adequately represented.

The examinations employed by different psychologists, schools, or medical centers differ considerably. None has been accepted as the "standard" against which all others are measured, nor does our theoretical understanding of the brain argue that any particular battery or test procedure is necessarily better than any other. Factors such as the proper use of tests, the ability of the clinician, and the appropriateness of the child determine the "rightness" of the battery in any given instance.

Despite these limitations, it is possible to discriminate a good set of tests from a bad set by becoming familiar with batteries of tests which have been generally accepted as comprehensive evaluations of the learning disabled child. One such battery has been described in the works of Ward Halstead (1947) and Ralph Reitan (1966).

The Halstead-Reitan Test Batteries

The Halstead-Reitan tests grew out of a massive research investigation into adult and child brain function initiated by Ward Halstead and carried on by his students, the foremost of whom has been Ralph Reitan. The work of these two men and their associates has produced a firm base which has significantly influenced the neuropsychological investigation of learning disabilities (Gaddes, 1968).

The battery consists of a number of tests, each of which is appropriate for a specified age range. Thus, children at different ages receive different tests. However, the tests are so structured as to yield a comprehensive examination for the child at each age level. Review of the tests in the battery will permit examination of the comprehensiveness required of a neuropsychological test battery.

TACTUAL PERFORMANCE TEST. In this test, the child is blindfolded and must place blocks into matching cut-out holes. For example, a star-shaped object must be placed in a star-shaped hole. However, since the child is blindfolded, this must be done entirely by touch. The test evaluates the child's ability to feel objects and recognize their shapes, to find the holes in the board in front of the child, and to get the shapes into the holes. The task is performed first with the dominant hand, then the nondominant hand, and finally with both hands. This produces a measure of the effectiveness of each hand as well as the ability of the child to learn as the test progresses. The test is appropriate for all ages, although children under nine use a simpler form of the test.

CATEGORY TEST. The Category Test is a test of concept formation. In the older children's version, the child is shown slides which suggest a number. For example, three blocks might suggest the number three. The child must guess which number is suggested, and pull one of four levers labelled from "1" to "4." If the correct lever is pulled, a bell rings; if the wrong lever is pulled, a buzzer is heard. In either case, the test moves ahead to another item which can be solved using the same idea as the previous items. In the example given here, the idea would be "the number to pull is the number of blocks present." This is a test of the child's ability to abstract rules from specific items and to learn by experience. It is also a measure of the ability to apply a general rule to different items. Overall, the test consists of several subtests, each of which uses a different basic principle.

For children under nine, a similar version of the test requires the child to guess colors rather than numbers.

SENSORY PERCEPTUAL EXAMINATION. This examination measures auditory, tactile, and visual skills through a series of subtests. The tactile area is covered most thoroughly, with tests evaluating the ability of the child to recognize numbers written on his or her fingers, identify which finger is touched, when blindfolded, and identify by touch simple objects placed in the child's hand. The tests also evaluate the functioning of the basic auditory and visual senses.

APHASIA EXAMINATION. This procedure evaluates all the major forms of aphasia (language disability). This includes the ability to read, to write, to name objects, to spell, to pronounce words, to explain phrases, to differentiate left from right, to identify body parts, to perform mathematics on paper and without paper, to demonstrate the use of an object not present, and to copy simple figures.

FINGER TAPPING TEST. The Finger Tapping Test measures the child's fine motor control by examining the speed at which the child can tap a telegraph key with each hand. The tapping is measured for ten seconds, and repeated five times for each hand.

SPEECH PERCEPTION TEST. This test plays a nonsense word from a tape. The child must match the word heard with several possible written words provided by the examiner on the test form. The test measures the child's ability to decipher a word phonetically and to then match the word to its written representation. The test is not used with children under nine.

RHYTHM TEST. In this test, a pair of rhythms are played from a tape. The child must identify whether the two rhythms are the same or different. Thirty pairs of items are presented. The test measures a child's ability to decode and retain rhythmic patterns, and then to compare two patterns against one another. The test is for children nine years old and up.

TRAIL MAKING TEST. The Trail Making Test consists of two parts. Part A consists of twenty-five circles distributed randomly on a page and numbered 1 to 25. The child must connect the circles in order. Part B consists of twenty-five circles which are numbered 1 to 13 or lettered A to L. The child must alternate between letters and numbers (1-A-2-B-3-C) when connecting the circles. The test measures spatial scanning, fine motor skills, counting, and flexibility in alternating tasks. The version for children aged nine to fourteen is somewhat shorter than the version above. The test is not given to children under nine.

MARCHING TEST. The Marching Test is a measure of a child's gross motor control. On sheets of paper the child must connect circles which vary from being in a straight line through those form patterns on the page. The test is done with the right and left hand individually. In an additional procedure, the child must mimic the arm and finger movements of the examiner. The examiner moves his fingers from circle to circle, alternating between the left and right hands. The child must follow these movements alternating his or her hands as well. The test is for children eight and younger.

COLOR FORM TEST. The Color Form Test provides a measure of a child's flexibility and abstractive ability. On the test the child must connect colored shapes, first by color then by shape. So, for example, the child moves from the red circle to the red square to the blue square to the blue triangle and so on. This color-shape alternation is similar to the letter-number alternation in the Trail Making Test above. The test is designed for children under nine.

PROGRESSIVE FIGURES TEST. This test attempts to measure the same skills as the Color Form Test in children under nine. The test consists of items with two shapes, a smaller one contained inside a larger one. The child must connect several such items, moving from the small shape inside to an identical larger shape. For example, one moves from a square within a circle to a triangle within the larger square. This test is a somewhat more difficult task than the color form test.

MATCHING FIGURES TEST. This procedure requires the child to match figures at the top of the page with figures at the bottom. At first, the figures at the top and bottom of the test are identical. In later items, the items are different although they are still in the same class of objects. For example, a candle might be matched to a light bulb since they both give light.

TARGET TEST. The apparatus for the Target Test consists of a card with nine circles arranged in three rows of three circles. The examiner points to a series of circles in a specific order. After a three second delay, the child must reproduce the pattern on a replica of the 3 by 3 inch grid placed before the child. The test is a measure of visual skills and memory as well as fine motor abilities.

INDIVIDUAL PERFORMANCE TEST. The Individual Performance Test consists of four measures of visual-spatial skills. In the first task, the subject must match a set of figures all shaped like *V*s by the angle of the two lines joined at the point of the *V*. A second measure involves the matching of complex, nonsense patterns. The third measure asks the subject to draw a series of squares, each inside the other. The fourth measure involves the drawing of a six-pointed star by drawing two triangles over one another. In each of the drawing tasks, the subject is shown how to do the drawing before being asked to do it. This is done in an attempt to reduce errors due to inexperience with similar figures.

WECHSLER INTELLIGENCE SCALES FOR CHILDREN. As the final testing procedure, the Wechsler Intelligence Scale for Children is administered in its entirety, as described in the last chapter. The WISC contributes a number of major measures including basic verbal skills, long and short memory, social awareness, fine motor skills, abstractive skills, and visual integrative abilities.

Validational Evidence

As can be seen from the description in the last few pages, the Halstead tests cover a wide range of abilities related to brain-based behaviors. However, this alone is not sufficient to establish the usefulness of a given test battery. Only the ability to show effective discrimination between brain injured and normal patients can fully validate a battery's usefulness.

The studies which have examined the Halstead-Reitan tests have been quite positive in supporting their usefulness and validity in detecting brain damage (Boll, 1974; Boll and Reitan, 1972, 1973; Klonoff and Low, 1974; Klonoff, Robinson, and Thompson, 1969; Reitan, 1974). Klonoff and his associates (1969) reported that the tests could accurately discriminate brain injury and normal patients over 80 percent of the time in three-year-olds and 96 percent of the time in children eight years old, when all the tests in the battery were used together. With children over nine years of age, Klonoff and Low (1974) reported an accuracy of 85 percent for the tests used altogether.

The most sensitive test—that is those which best discriminate between brain injured and normal children—were found to be the Progressive Figures Test, the Marching Test, and the Color Form Test (Reitan, 1974). In children nine and above, the most effective tests were the Trail Making Test and the Speech Perception Test (Boll, 1974). In both younger and older children, however, the tests in the WISC were in general more sensitive to brain damage than the Halstead-Reitan tests (Boll, 1974; Reitan, 1974).

Case Example

LX was an eight-year-old female who was performing normally in school. During a recess, she fell and knocked herself unconscious when her head hit the wooden corner of a sandbox. She was rushed to a hospital where it was found that there was bleeding under the surface of the skull just above the right eye. A subsequent operation corrected the medical problem, but LX was out of school for a period of eight months. Upon returning to school, she began to have significant problems with reading material she was once able to do and she seemed to have difficulty learning new material. She was still able to do work at the second and first grade level, except for a tendency to write letters backwards (b for d) and to misread letters. No deficits were found in intellectual testing. Some emotional problems were noted but none large enough to account for the child's problems in reading and writing.

Because of the history of brain damage, the child was referred for a neuropsychological evaluation. Overall, her performance was normal. However, she demonstrated some specific important deficits. Although she was able to repeat numbers told her, she was not able to do so when she had to repeat the numbers backwards. She showed some deficits on the *Progressive Figures Test* and the *Color Form Test*. She had difficulty with Part A of the *Trail Making Test* but not with Part B, suggesting some problem in spatial scanning rather than verbal alternation. No significant reading or writing problems were found, nor was she deficient in verbal intelligence (other than those described in the referral above). She exhibited some slowness in the left hand on finger tapping, but there were no sensory deficits in any modality.

Overall, this set of results suggested that there was a deficit in the right frontal area (third unit), which is characterized by difficulties in sequencing and abstract spatial problems. No verbal deficits were found, suggesting that the problem was not verbal but spatial. When reading, she had trouble staying on the correct line and moving from right to left. Rather than continuing to receive additional training in verbal skills, the child needed some aids which would indicate the direction to read across a line (provided by a space bar which could be moved down the page and which has an arrow pointing from left to right which the child could refer to). In addition, the bar allowed the child to see only one sentence at a time, stopping her wandering to other words on the page. With these aids, the child was able to read and quickly regained her past levels of reading. Over time, the aids were faded. Two lines of type at a time were exposed, then four, and so on until no additional aids of any kind were needed. The child is presently able to read without trouble.

Summary

The present chapter examines a typical comprehensive examination for possible brain injury. The Halstead-Reitan tests were used as the typical example. Each of the tests within the battery were described to illustrate the wide range of abilities tested in the comprehensive examination. Finally, a case example was presented to illustrate the usefulness of the Halstead-Reitan procedures in a learning disability case.

Chapter 13

HYPERACTIVITY:
DEFINITION AND DIAGNOSIS

H YPERACTIVITY is a symptom frequently associated with learning disabilities. In an extensive study of learning disabled
children, Hertzig, Bortner, and Birch (1969) found that nineteen
of ninety children with learning disabilities were hyperactive, a
rate of 21% or one out of every five. However, despite the common use of the term hyperactivity and the frequent diagnosis of
the condition, there have been problems in actually defining the
conditions.

Early definitions stressed the presence of excess activity in the
hyperactive child (Ounsted, 1955). In addition, authors suggested
additional symptoms such as short attention span, fluctuation
of mood, aggressive outbursts, lack of fear and shyness, excitability, neurological dysfunction, and other emotional or behavioral
problems (Werry, 1966; Ounsted, 1955). Despite clinical observations that such children are indeed more active (Chess, 1960;
Werry, 1968), there is little scientific evidence to support this
contention.

As a result many authors have stressed the quality of the motor
activity in the child rather than the quantity (Hutt and Hutt,
1964; Keogh, 1971; McFarland, Peacock, and Watson, 1966).
Thus, while the hyperactive child may not actually be more active
than other children, the child's behavior may be much more
socially inappropriate and irritating in the eyes of adults. As a
consequence, the behavior levels of such children become more
noticeable than in "normal" children.

Related Symptoms

Werry (1968) classifies five major classes of symptoms which may be associated with hyperactive children. However, it should be remembered that these symptoms may not necessarily occur in all children who are hyperactive.

ATTENTIONAL DEFECTS. Most observers of hyperactive children have suggested that they have very short attention spans. Such children are easily distracted and get involved in behavioral sequences which are unrelated to ongoing activity. Werry (1968) suggests that a related symptom is the tendency of the child to be impulsive and to fail to notice dangers in their environment.

EXCITABILITY. Stimuli which are pleasurable or frustrating may cause overreactions in hyperactive children (Werry, 1968). In general, their reactions exceed those which would normally be expected of a child the same age and sex.

LEARNING DISORDERS. Problems in learning are frequently associated with learning disabilities. In general, they are found to do poorly in school (Chess, 1960; Knobel, 1959, 1962; Keogh, 1971; Menkes, Rowe, and Menkes, 1967; Millichap, Aymat, Sturgis, Larsen, and Egan, 1968; Werry, 1968). Learning performance in these children may also vary on a day to day basis with little apparent consistency (Keogh, 1971).

There may be several reasons for this relationship. First, the very symptoms of constant inappropriate behavior and short attention span are clearly detrimental to adequate school performance. Thus, the child may have no cognitive disorders but simply fails to attend to the instruction and information necessary to successfully compete in school. A second possibility is that hyperactivity caused by brain damage may be associated with learning disorders caused by brain damage, depending on the size and location of the lesion. Finally, the child with a low frustration tolerance may simply be unable to withstand the pressures of making errors and learning more slowly than other children. Low frustration tolerance may lead to an inability to withstand failure of any kind, making learning nearly impossible.

NEUROLOGICAL DEFICITS. As with the learning disabled child, hyperactive children show more neurological symptoms in EEGs and neurological examinations (Werry, 1968). However, this is not because they are the same children as the children with learning problems. While the two groups overlap, they are in general quite distinct, especially when a learning disability is defined by the criteria presented in Section II. As in the case of the learning disabled children, the data is not absolutely confirmatory but clearly suggests a higher incidence of neurological dysfunction in hyperactive children.

EMOTIONAL DISORDERS.   Hyperactive children may show a number of emotional or behavioral problems, including defiance, aggressiveness, unpopularity with peers, and antisocial (criminal) behaviors (Werry, 1968). Hyperactivity is not necessarily associated with these disorders, and in general they appear to be the result of the child's upbringing, emotional stability, and family patterns more than a function of hyperactivity per se, as many hyperactive children are seen with none of these symptoms. As Werry points out, law enforcement agencies and mental health clinics are more likely to see the antisocial, disruptive hyperactive child rather than the pleasant hyperactive child, since the former is much more likely to be referred to social agencies than is the latter.

Etiology

As noted above, all learning disabled children are not hyperactive nor are all hyperactive children learning disabled. Similarly, all hyperactive children are not brain damaged nor all brain damaged children hyperactive. Hyperactivity may arise from a variety of sources, most important of which is serious emotional disorders. For example, a child from a poor home who feels abandoned may find hyperactivity the only way to get attention. Other children may find hyperactivity a good way of getting out of disagreeable tasks. Although these causes are not of primary interest to the current discussion, any diagnostic evaluation of the hyperactive child must rule out such possibilities.

ORGANIC ORIGINS.   As the reader may have noted, there are two important ways in which hyperactivity is linked to brain activity. This may be by damage to the first functional unit (Chapter 7) or the third functional unit (Chapter 9).

Damage to the first functional unit may lead to hyperactivity in two ways. First, the symptoms may arise from damage in the area of the hippocampus. Issacson (1974) has suggested that animals with hippocampal injuries are similar to normal animals who are easily frustrated. They become agitated and develop incorrect behavior when faced with any situation that does not deliver rewards regularly and frequently. In other words, they are unable to perform in situations in which the rewards are delayed or the rules of the situation are not spelled out clearly and concretely. Their behavior is marked by perseverative actions, in which a motor sequence is repeated endlessly. In the animal studies, the earlier the injury the higher the likelihood of hyperactivity. In addition, the presence of hippocampal injuries is associated with impairment of long-term verbal memories (especially if the injury is in the left hemisphere) but the perseveration of short-term memory is measured on the Digit Span task of the WISC. No other cognitive deficits are generally seen with these deficits, although diffuse motor and sensory impairment and other neurological signs may be present.

Hyperactivity may also arise through a dysfunction of the Reticular Activating System (RAS). Satterfield and Dawson (1971) found that many hyperactive children showed lower levels of basal skin conductance, as well as other measures which suggested a *lowered* level of basic physiological arousal in hyperactive children than in other children despite the suggestion of high arousal by their apparent level of activity. The authors theorized that this may be due to the lowered reactivity of the Reticular Activating System caused by a dysfunction related to an inherited disorder or brain injury. The authors suggested that hyperactivity in such children is secondary to the lowered level of Reticular Activating System arousal. The activity represents an attempt on the part of the brain to increase incoming stimuli to avoid a state of lowered sensory input. It is recognized that sensory deprivation of any kind is in general quite aversive to humans.

The RAS theory has the advantage of explaining why some hyperactive children respond well to stimulants. Stimulants raise the level of arousal in the RAS, hence reducing the need for stimulation from outside sources (moving around).

Hyperactivity may also arise from lesions of the third functional unit, the frontal lobe. If the frontal lobe connections between the first and third units are involved, this may lead to symptomology much like that found in first unit injuries since these connections play an important role in the Reticular Activating System. However, localized frontal lobe injuries will lead to more lateralized motor deficits than will first unit deficits. In addition, symptomology associated with frontal lobe learning disorders (Chapter 9) will also be present.

Patients with lesions to the prefrontal areas may be easily distracted by small noises or events that others are able to ignore. This symptomology is greater in the frontal lobe patient than in the patient with first unit lesions (Luria, 1966). These patients do quite well in situations where distractions are removed, while patients with first unit lesions, due to low levels of frustration tolerance, continue to react with what appears to be easy distractibility but is actually an attempt to avoid frustrations. Frontal patients are highly inflexible, and find it difficult to switch on command from one activity to another (Drewe, 1974; Milner, 1963). As in the case of other frontal lesions, there will be motor deficits which are usually lateralized and which are much more severe than any tactile deficits which may be present. Frontal patients are more likely to have severe cognitive deficits, especially when there is an early injury, as well as more labile (fluctuating) emotional states.

SECONDARY HYPERACTIVITY. In addition to hyperactivity directly related to brain damage as described above (primary hyperactivity), there is also the phenomenon of secondary hyperactivity. In these cases, the brain injury causes only cognitive deficits, usually involving the second unit. The injury interferes with the child's ability to learn, usually in verbal areas. (Lesions in the right hemisphere which do not affect verbal learning probably occur just as often but do not lead to the emotional reactions to be described.) The child enters school without a history of significant hyperactivity but begins to develop the disorder as soon as the learning material in school begins to frustrate him or her to the point where emotional problems begin to develop. Here we see the pattern of a child with normal or near normal development who appears to be well adjusted, only to develop hyperactive symptoms at school. In some cases, the symptomatology remains present only at school and in other cases begins to show up at home as well, but only after the school problems have become serious. This syndrome is characterized by poor attitudes towards schools and teachers and often by more acting out (destructive behavior) than is seen in children with other forms of hyperactivity. These children also have the ability to be still when they want to be, e.g. when watching television, usually a characteristic not seen in the other hyperactive children.

Secondary hyperactivity may occur as a result of frustrations other than a learning disability. For example, the poorly socialized child who is unable to get along with peers may develop similar symptoms. However, they will not show the cognitive symptoms of a second unit, localized disorder and generally will have a history of unsocialized behavior before beginning school.

Diagnosis

The diagnosis of hyperactivity due to brain injury is generally a subjective rather than an objective determination. As noted earlier, the actual level of behavior in the hyperactive child is not necessarily any greater than the level of behavior in any other child. Thus, level of activity alone cannot be used to make a distinction of hyperactivity. The diagnosis must rest upon the appropriateness of the child's behavior *as compared to the behavior of children the same age.* The age factor is an important one, since a four-year-old should not have to meet the expectations appropriate for an eight-year-old. In many cases, the diagnosis of hyperactivity results from parents' complaints when the real problem is the parents' intolerance of normal child behavior rather than inappropriate activity on the part of the child.

As a consequence, a diagnosis of hyperactivity cannot be accurately made solely upon the reports of parents or teachers. The diagnostician must see the child's behavior either at his or her office or, for best results, in a home and school visit. It is essential to establish that the hyperactivity occurs under many environmental conditions. If the child is only overactive at school, or only overactive at home, then it is likely that the problem is emotional rather than a dysfunction related to brain activity. One excellent time to evaluate the possibility of an emotional disorder is the activity of the child when he or she is watching a favorite television program or other activities the child especially enjoys. If the child is able to sit still for long periods of time under those conditions, the hyperactivity is not likely to be related to a brain dysfunction.

The history of hyperactive behavior is in the differential diagnosis of a brain dysfunction hyperactivity. The hyperactivity should be present from the time the brain injury occurred—at birth in most children. Hyperactivity which begins later and does not have a clear organic cause (head injury, for example) is likely due to emotional and environmental factors rather than organic, especially the type that begins during a significant change in the child's life (divorce of parents, death of parent, starting of school, birth of sibling, a significant emotional trauma from almost being killed, excessive fear, molestation, abandonment).

TYPE OF HYPERACTIVITY. Once it has been established that a child is likely to have a hyperactivity resulting from an organic brain dysfunction, it is appropriate to have the child fully evaluated for any motor, sensory, psychological, or neurological findings. The presence of these symptoms helps determine the type of activity manifested by the child. However, the presence or absence of these symptoms does not establish that any excessive behavior is organic hyperactivity. That must be done independently of the neurological evaluation as described above.

As noted before, hyperactivity related to injury in the first and third units is likely to be directly related to the brain injury rather than a secondary effect. In such children, diffuse motor and sensory problems are likely in third unit injuries. Third unit injuries may also be accompanied by a number of significant cognitive deficits and will be more pronounced in bilateral frontal injuries, which will be accompanied by bilateral motor deficits without sensory impairment.

Secondary hyperactivity related to second unit dysfunction will be accompanied by clear sensory and cognitive deficits related to dysfunction of the second unit. In addition, these children generally will not begin to show significant problems until beginning or well into school. It is important to distinguish between the types of hyperactivity as different treatments would theoretically be most applicable to each type (Section IV). However, in some cases there can be elements of each kind due to a more pervasive brain injury.

Summary

The present chapter examined the symptom of hyperactivity, which can occur by itself or along with clear deficiencies in learning skills. Hyperactivity may be due to brain injury or to significant emotional problems. It is a difficult disorder to define because many hyperactive children are not more active than other children but rather are more inappropriate in their behavior. Hyperactivity may be accompanied by a number of other symptoms including short attention span, excitability, and other behavior disturbances. Proper diagnosis requires a careful history and observation of a child, while psychological and neurological testing can aid in establishing the type of hyperactivity present.

Chapter 14

LIMITATIONS OF PSYCHOLOGICAL TESTING

T HE PREVIOUS chapters have placed a strong emphasis on the role of psychological testing in the evaluation of learning disabilities resulting from brain injury. The authors strongly feel that testing as described here offers the clearest possible picture of the learning disabled child, both for diagnostic purposes and for the design of rehabilitation programs. Despite this optimism, however, the authors recognize that there are significant limitations in the use of psychological tests with learning disabled children (as well as other children and adults). The major areas of caution for the user of psychological tests are outlined in the remainder of this chapter.

Testing the Hyperactive Child

Psychological testing is based on the assumption that individuals being tested will be motivated to do the best they can and will concentrate on the test and perform at the best of their abilities. This is not always true, especially when one is testing the hyperactive child. The child's constant restlessness, the inability to pay attention for long periods of time, the lack of motivation to do well on psychological tests, and other similar factors all interfere with test administration.

Consequently, it is quite possible that the child will not perform to the best of his or her ability. This is especially true on tests which require sustained concentration or when the child must keep track of previous items. For example, on the Category Test, what the child learns on the first items must be employed in the solution of subsequent items. However, if the child is restless and engages in a great deal of irrelevant activity, there is a much stronger possibility that the child will forget what has been previously learned. Under these circumstances the child is hampered in two ways. First, the extra activity itself interferes with memory. Secondly, the extra activity causes the test to last longer so that material must be remembered longer. The longer one needs to remember, the greater the amount of material forgotten. In the case of sustained attention tests, the child may be timed in completing a task like putting blocks together into a design. If the child engages in irrelevant activity, the completion increases and the child is likely to receive a lower score.

The effect of this situation is to cause the test to measure the child's behavior of the moment rather than the maximum ability of the child. Any conclusions reached under these conditions cannot be valid, as the interpretations for tests are dependent on the assumption that we are maximizing performance at the time of testing. This, in turn, makes conclusions and recommendations from the testing suspect, even when the tester attempts to estimate the child's potential skills by taking the distracting behavior into account. In actual practice, such "adjusting" is highly subjective and questionable. To avoid this, the tester attempts to use procedures which minimize the chance of the situation outlined above. Tests are used which minimize the need for sustained concentration or long-term memory. The child is constantly reinforced, using social as well as tangible rewards to keep the child from wandering and on task. The testing periods are kept short, and the child is allowed to discharge energy between the testing periods. The examiner attempts to build a close rapport with the child to increase cooperation (as is done with any child). Testing procedures may be slightly altered to allow for a better estimate of the child's performance, although this compromises the standardization of the test (Chapter 11).

Despite these procedures, there are children to whom it is simply impossible to give a valid standardized examination which can be interpreted according to the research on a given test. In this circumstance, the examiner must rely on qualitative rather than quantitative indicators to reach any conclusions. This is discussed in more detail later in this chapter.

The Emotional Child

The child who finds the testing situation frustrating may react with a number of emotional symptoms, ranging from refusing to do a test to actively destructive behavior. This clearly interferes with the validity of the test results as does the behavior of the hyperactive child described above. In these cases, the examiner must make a special attempt to establish a close rapport with the child to maximize cooperation. Often, this may necessitate a long period in which the examiner simply converses and plays with the child so that an atmosphere of trust may be created.

The examiner should attempt to create a rewarding atmosphere in which the child feels he or she is doing well no matter what the actual performance may be. Often children will be allowed extra time to finish tests so that they can have a sense of completion (although the extra performance is not counted in the scoring). In other tests, the task may be ended before it is scheduled to end to avoid the build-up of frustration. As in the case of the hyperactive child, test procedures may be altered to minimize problems.

Professional Credentials

The way of communicating test results in psychology and education leads to the unfortunate impression that the conclusions reached from testing are reached by the test itself. "The blank test indicated that Jody was learning disabled." Consequently it is important to remember that tests do not reach conclusions, people do. Tests serve only as sources of information which must be interpreted by a competent individual examiner if the results are to be meaningful. The interpreting individual reaches the final conclusions; consequently, the skills of the individual who makes the interpretations are as important or even more important than the actual tests given.

As a result, it is important to ensure that a sufficiently qualified individual interpret the testing. Unfortunately, it is difficult to identify who is a person qualified in the use of a particular test or test procedures, although minimal qualifications may be stated. For example, a psychologist using the neuropsychological techniques outlined in Chapter 12 (The Comprehensive Examination) should be well versed in brain function and the analysis of brain function. This should be shown by at least a year's experience under someone in the field and extensive background in the research involved in the area. Any individual offering neuro-psychological testing should be licensed for the practice of psychology. Individuals who are not licensed may not meet minimal standards to practice psychology in a given state. (Some individuals are allowed to practice without license in a number of states at the present time, although all states currently have licensing laws when this was written.) If a person is a psychologist, they should also be certified by the *National Register of Health Providers in Psychology,* a national organization attempting to identify psychologists with at least minimal competence to provide services to the public.

In choosing a school psychologist, the task is more difficult as strong licensing does not exist in all states. However, school psychologists should be licensed in states where it is required and certified by the state's department of education (or the equivalent) to practice school psychology. The individual should have, as a minimum, a masters degree in school psychology and, preferably, a doctorate of education degree. The more training an individual has in the specific area in which a child has problems, the better the person is likely to do his or her job.

It is recognized that the requirements given above do not necessarily mean that a person will do the best job, nor will the person without them necessarily be unable to do the job. However, setting standards for training and experience helps ensure the minimum competencies considered appropriate in a field. Parents faced with the decision of whom to see would best talk over their needs with a local university or college department of psychology or psychiatry, with friends in similar situations, and with other knowledgeable individuals such as a neurologist or a family physician who has seen the child.

Qualitative versus Quantitative Interpretations

So far in this book we have emphasized the need for tests which are standardized, quantitative, and have a strong research background. However, we have also noted the importance of the skills of the individual examiner and the inability to use standardized tests and procedures in some difficult testing situations. It is often the case that the insight of the individual examiner, properly verified by test results, can produce many more important results than standardized test procedures alone. However, insight in a given examiner cannot be taught and at best is difficult to determine. When present, such insight can be especially valuable; when absent, it can cause a set of test results to be misinterpreted.

Interpretations based on factors other than quantitative numbers are qualitative in nature. When looking for qualitative results, the examiner can change test procedures or scoring rules and can invent procedures on the spot for the individual child as demanded in the unique individual case. As stated above, this can be a very powerful approach but only when done by an individual who is highly knowledgeable and experienced. Only such an individual is fully able to appreciate the changes in performance to be expected when one changes test procedures and makes changes on the basis of logical, theoretical reasons rather than random changes or those made capriciously or accidentally by the inexperienced examiner.

Prognosis and Prediction

One nagging question in the field of learning disabilities is the question of why some children spontaneously get better while others do not seem to improve. As can well be understood, it is important to know which group a child belongs to. If the child will improve on his or her own, the need for rehabilitation services or special classes is minimized. However, if the problem will not improve or might even get worse, it is necessary to insure that such a child gets all the help needed. Unfortunately, at the present time there is no clear way of making such predictions.

Some general ideas about this can be gained from the testing. In general, those test results which suggest developmental delay in general rather than brain injury indicate the child will recover with age. When such a delay is an important factor in the child's disorders, care should be taken that the child does not become frustrated with his or her inability to match age peers in performance. This can cause emotional problems which interfere seriously with later development. In some cases, however, the apparent delay is due to brain injury of a diffuse nature which is missed. These children do not show the strong catch-up abilities of the developmentally delayed child. This distinction can be difficult to make in some cases but is important. As a rule, we treat children who have a possibility of brain injury by offering rehabilitative help to avoid missing a child who might seriously need help. However, we make it clear to parents that the condition may clear up on its own.

Where evidence suggests an old focal disorder, our experience has been that there is little spontaneous recovery, although such children will improve with age through the improvement of other, alternative skills. Appropriate rehabilitation should be immediately started with any child with a test pattern indicating focal problems.

Again, the guidelines presented above are general and not absolute. Factors in individual cases may change one's impression about what is likely to occur in the future. Much more extensive research is needed so that we can become more accurate in our predictions and in selecting the appropriate children for special services.

Testing Minority Children

The testing of minority children has become a controversial issue in psychology and education. In recent years, many school districts have abandoned IQ testing and similar tests because of protests by parents and educators that such tests were only useful for white middleclass children. Although the IQ controversy is not directly related to the questions of brain damage, it clearly signals an area in which we must be cautious.

Most tests specifically designed for learning disabled children share the flaw of being appropriate for only white children, and few have the research necessary to validate their use with the minority child. Children with low socioeconomic status have been shown to do quite poorly on a number of tests used for learning disabilities, even those like the Bender-Gestalt which only require a drawing response (Amante and others, 1977; Birch and Gussow,

1970; Pasamanick and Knoblock, 1961; Small, 1973; Wender, 1971).

The deficit does not hold for all tests. Tests in the Halstead-Reitan battery have generally been found to be useful in different cultural groups ranging from American Indians to Swedish patients (Golden, 1978; Klove, 1974; Luria, 1966, 1973). On the WISC, test scores on the performance tests appears equal in many groups while test performance on the verbal tests may be significantly lower in minority groups (Golden, Roraback, and Prey, in press).

There have been recent attempts to develop tests more appropriate for minority populations (for example, Williams, 1975). These tests have not yet been extended into the area of learning disabilities, but probably will in the future. At the present time, one is restricted to the tests available. Consequently, it is incumbent on the user to employ tests which are least affected by culture, and to interpret test results cautiously in minority children.

Summary

The chapter examines issues which limit or affect the uses of psychological tests in the evaluation of children. Both hyperactivity and the inability to withstand frustration can interfere with test results, making it difficult to get valid results. The examiner needs to use techniques to minimize the behavior problems of such children including building a strong rapport, short testing sessions, judicious selection of tests, and so on. Test users should insure that the examiner is a competent and licensed psychologist, as the selection of examiner and interpreter of test results is highly critical. Experienced examiners may employ qualitative techniques in addition to quantitative techniques, but these can be dangerous in the hands of the inexperienced examiner. While tests attempt to make predictions about the future, there are currently great shortcomings in the procedures. Finally, test results of minority children must be treated cautiously and an attempt must be made to avoid test bias in such children.

Section IV

REHABILITATION

Chapter 15

REHABILITATION IN LEARNING DISORDERS

D ESPITE THE EXTENSIVE INTEREST in the rehabilitation of the learning disabled child, there is little if any significant research which concentrates on relating the individual injuries of the brain injured child, ascertained in a systematic and reliable manner, to specific teaching techniques. In general, most research has looked at the effect of one technique or sets of techniques on groups of children diagnosed as learning disabled, reading retarded, hyperactive, or the like. While such research clearly has its uses, it limits us greatly in attempting to work from the problems of the specific brain injured child to an individualized program. It should be noted that individualized does not mean each student works alone at different levels of the same teaching material, but that the specific material chosen for each child is individualized for that child's needs.

This chapter will concentrate on what kinds of considerations need to be addressed in devising a program for the specific child, emphasizing the limitations of each approach. As we shall see, many of the decisions which need to be made depend on the goals one wishes to set for a child as much as the actual nature of the child's disabilities. Although the present authors have clear biases when these questions arise, they are decisions which must be made by the joint considerations of the parents and teachers involved with a specific child.

The Role of Diagnosis

As has been emphasized throughout this volume, the importance of differential diagnosis cannot be underestimated in treating the learning disabled child. These children often have complex, subtle problems which cannot be easily understood under broad terms like "auditory learner" or "'visual learner." As we have seen, the brain is a highly complex and interdependent organ, and the nature of the problems in children with similar overt behavior may differ considerably. Thus it is imperative that any rehabilitation plan begin with an adequate diagnostic evaluation to pinpoint as closely as possible the nature of the child's disorder. Although precise results are not always possible in every child due to individual factors, the examination must give us an understanding of the general extent of any brain injury present and its relationship to the development of functional systems within the brain.

Approaches to Rehabilitation

There are four major ways to approach the child or adult with brain injury (Luria, 1963). These approaches are (1) direct retraining of the lost skill; (2) substitution of alternate basic skills for a lost skill; (3) substitution of more complex skills for a lost skill; and (4) environmental changes.

DIRECT RETRAINING. Direct retraining involves the substitution of another part of the brain for an injured area or the retraining of the injured area itself. Retraining of the injured area is only possible when damage to an area responsible for a given skill has been only partial. For example, partial injury to the temporal lobe might interfere with a child's ability to understand speech sounds. If the injury is only partial, however, the child would be able to gain the skill with extensive training of the area by repeatedly going over the basic ability involved.

Takeover by another part of the brain may occur in two ways. First, the opposite hemisphere of the brain, if intact, may be able to take over the function of the injured area if the brain injury occurs early enough. This, however, is not likely in later injuries. The second method of takeover occurs in complex skills which involve both hemispheres. For example, both the right and left hemisphere are closely involved with most spatial functions. If a right hemisphere injury occurs, extensive improvement can be gained by allowing the left hemisphere to take over the functions of the injured hemisphere. This could be done, for example, by encouraging the patient to think of spatial tasks in verbal terms. This will cause the left hemisphere to become more heavily involved and will aid in the transfer of the task. With extensive repetition the task will become automatic and the verbal mediation can drop out.

The approach works by directly challenging a weak spot in the student's skills. In many ways, this is a difficult approach to use. The student will seemingly make less progress than with the other methods because of the need to build up a skill not already present, rather than use a skill already available as other techniques may. The advantage of the approach is that it enables the student to eventually function at as normal a level he or she is capable of attaining, given the limitations of the injury, general motivation, and general intelligence. This approach offers the child more alternatives later in life since there is not a glaringly weak area in the child's skills.

On the negative side, as has been stated, this technique is more difficult and is slower than other techniques. It requires significantly more patience on the part of the child, the teacher, and parents. They must be willing to settle for long-term modest goals rather than dramatic "improvements." The child may have to accept that he or she must work harder at something than other children, and practice at tasks that are so basic as to seem "childish."

In general, these techniques are best used in the cases of highly delimited disorders in young children. In a highly delimited disorder, the prognosis for these methods is good and the end result is a child who is essentially normal in skills. In younger children, there is no problem with the child seeing the task as "childish" nor with encouraging the work with proper social and tangible rewards which young children thrive on. With young children, there is also a higher chance of success.

As a rule, these techniques are contraindicated in children with more massive injuries and those who are older, especially when the disorder has existed for a long period of time. Older children are often impatient for results, and so these techniques are not as effective. Children with massive injuries generally face too many separate disorders for the approach to be successful.

The most common example of these techniques involves the teaching of phonemic analysis to the language retarded child with a basic disorder in phonemic analysis. At first, a child is taught to discriminate between pairs of phonemes said by the teacher which are not similar *(t* and *m* for instance). As the child becomes more proficient, training extends to phonemes which are highly similar *(t* and *d).* After the initial phase is over, the child must discriminate sounds played on a tape recorder, a task which is considerably more difficult. After this is accomplished, the child is moved to two syllable words, then to saying the phonemes (although this is sometimes useful in the first stage as well unless there is a speech difficulty) and finally to discriminating among full words. Each of these stages may last a considerable period of time and each is accompanied by extensive practice.

SUBSTITUTION OF MORE BASIC SKILLS. This technique involves the use of simpler skills which can be put together to make up a more complex skill. In injuries to the third functional unit, for example, we often see impairment of planning skills, decision making ability, organizational ability, and the like. For these children, we can substitute skills of which they are capable. For example, if a child could read, he or she could be given a list of rules to follow in a given situation. A list of rules might include the following: "When you come to the corner, stop. Look each way for a car. If you see one, don't go on. When you no longer see a car, cross the street." In the child without a third unit injury, such a sequence eventually would become an automatic part of the judgment decisions we call "common sense." The injured child is not capable of this and may always have to refer to such memorized or written sets of instructions. However, the technique has the advantage of allowing the child or adult to function within a defined set of environmental conditions. This technique is most applicable to frontal lobe (third unit) injuries. They are applicable no matter what the degree of injury. In the case of lesser injuries, there will eventually be less and less reliance on the steps as the skills become automatic. In more severe injuries, the patient will remain dependent on the steps. The nature of the patient's response to the technique must be considered carefully in any career planning for the individual.

In a second unit disorder, this technique can also be useful. Luria (1966) gives the example of the man unable to pronounce the letter *p*. However, the man was able to blow a flame out. Using this basic blowing movement, the patient was eventually able to produce the *p* sound.

SUBSTITUTION OF MORE COMPLEX SKILLS. Just as we can break a complex skill into more basic parts, we can make a basic skill part of a more complex process. For example, in the case of a pure dyslexic child with auditory-verbal disconnections, reading could be taught by associating intact phonemic sounds with letters felt by hand. These tactile letters could then be associated with their visual counterparts. Eventually, this would lead to teaching the child to associate a letter's visual and auditory components with the tactile intermediate in memory. With time, a child trained in this method can read without using the image of the tactile letters. Indeed, this technique has been used successfully with many pure dyslexic children. However, it will only work well in the case of a lesion confined to the auditory-verbal areas which does not invade the auditory-tactile or tactile-visual areas of the second unit of the brain.

This approach may be used in other ways as well. A child having problems with tapping sequences may not be able to tap a series of four taps, but may be able to tap the sum of two plus two. The second task involves higher centers of the brain, while the first demands a basic rhythmic analytic skill. With training, the two can be combined so that the child is eventually able to complete the rhythmic pattern.

This approach is most useful with children who have limited but complete injuries which make the first technique unusable. Clearly, forming complex chains and relationships within the brain is difficult, as numerous separate skills must be practiced. However, this can result in a complete absence of later deficit if planned properly, an important factor in the program of any child. As with the first technique, this technique is difficult to use with older children or those with more extensive brain injury.

This approach is usually not as difficult as the first method in that the weak area is not directly attacked, thus avoiding the frustration of working on a difficult task to improve skill.

REDEFINING THE TASK. This does not involve a rehabilitation of the child. It utilizes changing the environment to fit the child, rather than changing the child to fit the environment. According to this approach, if a child cannot read because of visual problems, the child should learn by listening instead. If a child cannot learn from hearing things, let him or her read rather than attend lectures. This approach has clear advantages to the school system. Instead of requiring remedial help, it requires only efforts by personnel to identify the "channel" the child learns through and then to provide the appropriate material. If the learning disability is indeed specific, the environmental approach can often be effective in allowing the child to learn at his or her expected rate.

The problem with this approach is that there is no remediation. The child continues to have serious learning limitations which may limit future job alternatives and general career decisions. This is justified by some because they feel that remediation, as has been described here, is neither possible nor profitable. While this is probably true for some children, it is not true for all children. Again, a detailed evaluation is needed so we can determine the chance that remediation efforts will improve a child's basic functioning before we abandon all such approaches. This alternative is useful in the case of the older child whose behavioral problems or level of frustration preclude remediation, or the child whose problems are so serious or so complete as to make remediation essentially impossible. This method should never be used, however, simply because it is more convenient for school personnel or for the parents.

Determining Task Content

Determining task content depends upon the goals of the testing program. It is important to recognize that theoretically one can include just about any appropriate content in given task for spatial or other type of problems. An individual can learn to put a puzzle together as one form of a spatial task or learn to write a line straight across the page as another form. Because of the importance of the training to educational goals, we usually try to include content that is relevant to current school tasks. For example, visual discrimination will focus on discriminating different letters from one another. Frontal lobe planning skills might deal with the organization of an essay or the telling of a story. In each case we strengthen not only the neuropsychological ability that we are working on but also related academic skills as well. This allows for faster progress and more enthusiasm on the part of teacher and student. In general, we discourage programs which work on material which is not ultimately related to the skills the child needs for academic or vocational training.

Determining Priorities

In most children, there is more than one set of remedial tasks which one would like to train the child. In these cases, one must assign priorities to the tasks in order to begin therapy. We prefer to minimize the number of areas a child is working in, as we have found that concentrated attention in a single area is likely to yield more effective results than programs which divide activities into small periods of concentration on a wide variety of tasks.

In determining priorities, one must take several factors into account. First, training should begin on the skills involving the most basic deficits as these are necessary for training more complex tasks. Second, one attempts to choose tasks that are most educationally relevant to the child and his or her current curriculum. Third, it is helpful to pick those areas where there are deficits obvious to the child but which can be easily remediated. This allows for early success and a higher motivation level for the child, parents, and teachers.

These priorities may often conflict with one another and decisions must be made on an individual basis. None of the principles is more important than the others in a given situation. For example, a child who has been frustrated by failure in school and who shows low motivation would best be served by using the third principle. A child just beginning school without having a history of failure (because of noninvolvement in school tasks) would best be helped by invoking principle two. A child with numerous deficits would best be approached by principle one in the absence of a history of emotional problems due to frustration. The effects of each choice should be carefully considered for the individual child, with the decision made on what will optimize the training in the long run.

Task Construction

There are five major considerations in the design of rehabilitation tasks: (1) The task should include the impaired ability, but no other impaired skill. For example, if a child has impaired motor and receptive speech, a task for receptive speech should not include motor speech, as this doubles the task difficulty and can often confuse the child. (2) The task designed should vary from very simple levels to complex levels on a graduated scale which allows small increases in difficulty as a child progresses. This is an aid in avoiding jumps in complexity which may be too large and which may confuse or frustrate the child. (3) The task should be objectively assessed in some manner so both the teacher and student are aware of progress. Such assessments should be done frequently so that progress can be used as a reinforcer. This also allows continued evaluation of a task. If no progress is seen in the child's skills, the task is either too easy, too hard, or inappropriate in some manner. (4) The task should involve immediate feedback to the child. The child should know whether a given response was right or wrong. If wrong, the reason for this should be obvious or should be stated to the child. Only through constant, accurate feedback can one learn to modify behavior in a correct manner. Tasks which are difficult to assess immediately should be avoided as well as those for which it is difficult to give accurate immediate feedback. (5) Tasks should be constructed to avoid frequent errors on the part of the child in an effort to maintain motivation. However, they should not be so easy as to provide no challenge or sense of accomplishment.

Secondary Emotional Problems

Before ending this chapter on rehabilitation, it is necessary to address the problem of secondary emotional problems. These problems are called "secondary" because they are not caused by the brain injury, but by reactions to the resulting disability. These problems can persist long after the cause has disappeared or be cleared up on their own while the disability remains. In many children who are exposed to early failure, it is this feeling of failure, of being "no good," rather than the inability to remediate a specific learning disability, that dooms rehabilitation programs.

Because of the effects these problems have on learning and on the child's social relationships, it is often neecssary that they be treated. This treatment can range from counseling at school to family or individual therapy at a mental health clinic or with a private psychologist or psychiatrist. The types of therapy advocated by different practitioners is quite variable depending on the orientation of the practitioner. Research in therapy seems to suggest that no one form of therapy is superior for everyone. Rather one should work with an individual one can trust and communicate with who has had proper training in doing psychotherapy as evidenced by state licensure, as well as the other qualifications listed earlier in this book. Having found an acceptable individual or approach, it is important to stay with the therapy and work at it even when one is faced with difficult issues that may be painful to examine.

Summary

The present chapter examined a rehabilitation approach consistent with the theoretical and assessment approaches discussed in this book. The role of the diagnostic evaluation in determining specific remediational goals was emphasized. The four ways to approach a rehabilitation problem were discussed: building up a weak skill, substituting more basic skills, substitution of more complex skills, and redefinition of the task. The use of educational goals to define task content was advocated. The major methods of determining rehabilitation priorities require consideration of the basic nature of the skill, its role in school curriculum, and its effect on the child's overall motivation. Finally, the importance of recognizing and treating secondary emotional disorders was briefly presented.

Chapter 16

REHABILITATION TECHNIQUES

A s WE NOTED in the last chapter, there are numerous rehabilitation tasks which can be designed for the individual child. As
a rule, these techniques can involve easy to make materials or
standardized materials available from a number of educational
suppliers in the areas of special education. As a consequence, we
do not advocate standard techniques, but rather urge users of
these ideas to design their own material to fit the needs of the
child and the resources available. Consequently, the following
techniques should be considered as only suggestions rather than
the "correct" techniques for a given problem.

In order to provide a clear focus to this chapter, we will deal
with the treatment of injuries that directly affect academic skills
and suggestions for remedial tasks will deal specifically with that
area. While other alternatives for training are available in designing an individualized program, it is our feeling that techniques oriented toward school deficits will yield faster and more
satisfactory results.

Motor Disorders

Motor disorders may arise from lesions to the third brain unit
or may be the result of sensory problems, which will be dealt with
later. Motor problems are especially serious in their effect on the
ability of the child to write. A child may be able to read and
show normal language development, but find it impossible to
write. As a rule, these are disorders of fine motor skills. In children where the problems are confined to one hand, it is most common to allow the opposite hand (whether or not it is dominant)
to take over writing tasks. While this may be somewhat awkward
at first, especially in the older child, normal writing practice will

eventually yield normal writing skills.

If the child is impaired in both hands or there is a reason for using the impaired hand, then it is best to use one of several techniques which help guide the child in his or her writing. One task uses preprinted letters which the child traces. As time goes on and the child's proficiency increases, the letters are printed more lightly and eventually only parts of the letters are presented. One commercially available technique uses a special pen and paper. When the child writes correctly, the paper allows a line to be printed; when the child goes off the correct place for the letter, the line shown is much lighter, indicating an error. At first, the child traces letters which are slowly faded out over time.

In the past five years, there have been a number of electronic devices introduced with the same primary function. When the child writes or draws incorrectly while using a special electronic pen, a buzzer is sounded allowing the child to correct himself. As with the above techniques, these devices may allow a child first to trace and later to draw freehand.

Motor problems may affect reading skills as well when the child has specific problems with eye movements. Reading requires successive serial fixations of the eye across the page. When these cannot be performed, the child may read backwards, skip words, read only parts of words, skip lines, or randomly fixate across a page. Clearly, any of these conditions can interfere with reading skills.

This problem may be attacked in several ways. A number of therapists offer treatment which allows a child to follow a moving target. These, however, are better suited for control of eye movements in general rather than reading in particular. Reading involves a fairly predictable, sequential series of fixations. Simple reading material with several large words on a line (for example, books for individuals with visual problems) can be used. A cardboard mask can also be used. At first the mask allows one word on one line to be seen at a time. After the child is proficient at following this, several words at a time may be exposed. Later, additional lines may be exposed or smaller print employed. With repeated practice at each step, the child can continually improve his or her skills. In the case of children with right-left orientation problems, an arrow pointing to the right which is quite conspicuous can be placed on the mask to indicate direction. In later work, this arrow can be reduced in size until it is eliminated.

Auditory Disorders

Disorders of the auditory receptive areas in both hemispheres can cause total deafness. An injury destroying the receptive area in the left hemisphere in an older child will result in pure word deafness, the loss of the ability to hear verbal sounds. In younger children, similar results may occur but there is more likelihood of takeover by the right hemisphere. No psycho-educational treatment for total deafness is possible, but the treatment for all lesser conditions is the same. The child must be repetitively drilled to differentiate between English phonemes, starting with those that do not sound alike (*f* and *g*) and eventually working on those that do sound alike (*d* and *t*). During the first phase the child should be able to watch someone say the word and be instructed to repeat them or point to the letter on a chart. After this is completed, the child should learn to discriminate without being able to watch the person saying the word. Later, the child should be taught to discriminate from a tape recorder. This treatment is the technique of choice in any disorder affecting phonetic understanding. In some cases, this results in retraining remaining intact areas in the injured hemisphere. In some cases it involves the opposite hemisphere and in some children there is a blending of visual (seeing the word said) and auditory areas.

Auditory-Visual Areas

Lesions to these areas cause pure dyslexia, the complete inability to read in the absence of all other symptoms. The treatment for this has been described in the last chapter and involves a matching of auditory to tactile figures and tactile to visual figures with eventual training in auditory to visual figures.

Verbal-Spatial Deficits

Lesions of the integrative areas of the left hemisphere may cause deficits in the understanding of words denoting relationships, especially prepositions such as *below*. Treatment of this disorder is through associating pictures representing the word and an explanation of the relationship, thus involving right hemisphere and frontal rather than parietal areas of the left hemisphere in the task. In early stages of this training, the child may be asked only to differentiate between opposites (above and below). Later the child is asked to choose from more alternatives and finally must generate the word spontaneously. An additional advanced technique is to tell the child the word and allow the child to put together an appropriate picture.

Abstraction (Categorization) Problems

Abstract thinking involves the ability to classify objects as the same or different on the basis of qualities or dimensions that two or more objects have in common. These abilities are essential both to memory functions (which use classifications apparently to store ideas) and to higher abstract, intellectual skills. Classification skills are taught by repeated exercises in the deficit area. As a rule this starts out by giving the child chips, blocks, pictures, or some other material that can be divided into two groups in several different ways. The early tasks involve giving the child objects which can be categorized, e.g. objects which are red. Then the work can be extended by giving another category, e.g. shape. When the child is able to do this reliably, then the child may be taught to generate his or her own category problems using the same materials at first and different materials later. After this is achieved, work may be done with categories containing from three groups up to about five groups. The task can be made harder or easier by using either concrete words with clear real world reference, e.g. a ball, or by using abstract words, e.g. liberty, without clear objective meanings.

Sequencing Deficits

Sequencing deficits may arise out of a number of basic disorders: (1) a verbal inability to link objects by a logical story; (2) an inability to keep things in sequence that have a specific order; and (3) an inability to remember objects in a sequence. The verbal deficit, the inability to link discrete events within a single story, is usually associated with lesions in the frontal lobes (third unit). The basic training for this deficit consists of two parts: (1) observing the actions and possibilities within a single picture or situation and (2) fitting a series of pictures within a reasonable story line. The first goal requires the child to examine the contents of a picture, the relationship of the objects within the picture, and to speculate on the possible antecedents and consequences of the actions within a picture. It is typical of the brain injured child to concentrate on describing objects within the picture while omitting information about possible actions or interactions among the segments within a picture.

The training task should encourage the child to develop such information by providing the kind of questions or program the patient should be asking of himself. It is often useful to do the steps for the child first, slowly letting the child learn to ask the questions himself or herself. This allows an essentially "higher" skill to be replaced by a series of simpler skills. In working with a child, the teacher should provide maximum feedback to show the adequacy of the child's responses and to show alternate things the child could have looked at. Such help should be at a level compatible with the child's social and intellectual maturity.

The second step in developing sequencing is to give the subject a series of pictures, starting with two, that can be arranged in only one logical order. It is the patient's responsibility to make up a logical story that allows him or her to put the pictures in the correct order. If an incorrect story is given because something has been ignored, the child is informed that this is the case and asked to try again. If there is considerable trouble, the child should be given hints until the skill is further developed.

Speech Deficits

Speech deficits may arise from lesions of the tactile areas of the brain which interfere with a child's ability to locate his tongue and lips accurately in the formation of speech sounds. In these disorders, the patient has a great deal of difficulty with sounds produced by similar muscular movements. Training in this area involves feedback to the patient to supplant the feedback which has been disrupted. This is most effectively done through allowing the patient to observe his or her own progress in a mirror and to hear the sounds produced on a tape recorder. Training should initially involve those phonemes easy for the patient, progressing to those which are found to be more difficult.

Lesions in motor speech areas can produce complete paralysis of the speech apparatus. In less severe cases, however, there may be the ability to say simple phonemes but not the ability to say complex words. The child may have trouble switching from one sound to another, leading to preseveration. In more severe cases, speech may be started by using basic skills. For example, as was noted before, the letter *p* may be started by using a blowing response. It is also useful to allow the child to watch his or her motor movements of the mouth in a mirror as a further aid. In less severe cases, where the patient has difficulty putting sounds together in a sequence, the introduction of a second element in the speech process may be helpful. For example, the patient could be taught to say a syllable after squeezing a fist or blinking an eye, thus adding pacing and other intact motor functions to the speech process. With training, the time between syllables can be reduced and the extra movement eventually eliminated.

Memory Disorders

The loss of verbal memory skills can lead to a great number of obvious symptoms. The basic rehabilitation strategy is to build upon the resources of the brain as a whole to take over memory functions. The process is begun with simple memory problems (one element) and increased to more complex memory problems (five to seven elements) with training. If the memory impairment is selective—either verbal or nonverbal—the impaired memory may be improved by associating words with pictures and having the child learn to memorize the easier set. The more difficult set can then be attempted by learning to translate from one form of memory to the next. Various techniques used by mnemonic experts are available in book form and can also be used with older children. Categorizing skills, if deficient, can also impair memory function. Consequently, teaching categorization can be useful in improving memory.

Visual Disorders

Visual-letter agnosia occurs as the result of left occipital injuries. In this disorder, the child, while able to see perfectly well, is unable to appreciate the meaning of letters and may be unable to discriminate them as anything but patterns of lines. One helpful treatment for this disorder is to allow the patient to construct replicas of letters from toothpicks or other materials while working on the auditory meaning of the letters. This technique involves intact spatial skill areas of the right hemisphere.

In less severe forms the patient may be able to appreciate what a letter is and be able to recognize letters. However, this can be done with only one letter at a time. Consequently, the patient is able to read only very slowly and may lose the beginning of a word before reaching the end. These individuals are able, however, to learn sight reading (reading words as a single unit rather than a collection of letters). They are only able to read one word at a time, but this is a significant improvement over their apparent complete dyslexia when forced to learn by phonetic methods.

In disorders of the right hemisphere occipital lobe, the patient may ignore the entire left half of the page. For example, the patient would only see the right half of each line on this page and is often unable to appreciate that something has been missed. For such patients, an anchor or arrow indicating where to begin reading (or writing) is useful in keeping the patient aware that they are not at the proper place. In more severe cases, a graduated ruler can be used. The patient is required to move from 1 to 2 to 3 and so on as he goes across the page each time. (The ruler may also be used for children with left-right disorders.)

Mathematical Deficiencies

Mathematical disorders resulting from left hemisphere injuries in the second unit are a result of the inability to understand the spatial nature of mathematical operations. While the individual can learn counting, the child finds any operation such as addition impossible. In these cases, it is important to relate the operations repeatedly to their concrete representations. For example, addition is simply putting five sticks and four sticks together and counting the result. Subtraction is taking sticks away and so on. Unlike normal children, children with this disorder need these examples drilled repeatedly. These children can also be helped by learning basic mathematical facts by rote memory, rather than expecting them to figure things out by logic.

Summary

This chapter explored various possible training techniques for specific disorders which interfere with school skills. As can be seen, none of the techniques need to involve complex apparatus and many can be recognized as techniques in common use although not always for the purposes suggested here. As noted in the previous chapter, none of the techniques themselves are unique nor are they intended to be. Each is appropriate for a specific kind of disorder as illustrated in the chapter.

Chapter 17

THE TREATMENT OF HYPERACTIVITY

T HE TREATMENT of hyperactivity has been one of the most controversial issues in the area of learning disabilities. The major problems have centered around the decision to use stimulant drugs to control the behavior. The question of drug use has elicited extreme responses from both proponents and opponents. Respected authorities both in and out of medicine can be quoted on both sides of this often confusing issue. The present chapter will attempt to briefly summarize the information available and to draw some general guidelines of use for the nonphysician.

Drug Treatment

HISTORICAL DEVELOPMENT. Early research on the use of stimulant drugs in the treatment of hyperactive behavior can be traced to the work of Bradley (1937) who observed, in a largely uncontrolled study, the beneficial effects of a stimulant drug in children with behavioral disorders. Bradley found positive results in about half of his thirty children. By 1950, Bradley was ready to conclude that about 50 to 60 percent of children with behavior problems improve on amphetamines, while 15 to 25 percent show no change, and 10 to 15 percent actually get worse. Bradley's research efforts set a pattern of results that have been repeated in a number of studies.

Denhoff, Davids, and Hawkins (1971), in a well-controlled double-blind study, found improvement in twenty-seven of forty-two children when they were on a stimulant as compared to when they were on a nonworking drug called a placebo. In a double-blind situation, neither the child nor the experimenter, parents, or teachers know what drug he or she is on. Thus, the assessment of the child's behavior is made without the person watching the child knowing whether the child is on the drug. This makes the assessment more objective and precludes bias toward or against the drug. It should be noted, however, that double-blind studies of this kind are rarely perfect. The drugs involved may frequently cause side effects in children, creating signs that can be seen by a knowledgeable observer.

In a similar study, Steinberg, Troshinsky, and Steinberg (1971) found more improvement in twenty-five of forty-six children than was found with a placebo. The authors observed that their best results were found in children with one hard neurological sign or several soft neurological signs, those children who are the most likely to be brain injured in the first or third units. Other studies have also reported positive results for the drug treatment of hyperactivity (Sprague, Barnes, and Werry, 1970; Huestis, Arnold, and Smeltzer, 1975; Eisenberg, Conners, and Sharpe, 1975). Epstein, Lasagna, Connors, and Rodriguez (1968) found that children with a history of brain injury responded better to the drug treatment than children without a history of such damage.

ADVERSE EFFECTS. In addition to the positive effects of the drug treatment, there are also negative effects that have been reported in the literature. As noted earlier, Bradley (1957) reported that between 10 and 15 percent of his children across a number of studies actually got worse while on the drug. Other authors have reported a variety of disorders in treated children including movement disorders, worse hyperactivity, loss of appetite, inability to sleep, dizziness, and other similar symptoms (Grinspoon and Singer, 1973). Of special interest are several studies which have suggested a loss of weight and a cessation of growth in children on drugs for a long period of time. These studies have reported that children will lose weight while on significant doses of medication, and that this will be followed by a lack of growth as measured by height (Safer, Allen, and Barr, 1972; Sleator and von Neurmann, 1974). These effects of long-term usage necessitate caution in the use of many of these medications, even in children who are helped by the drug.

Guidelines for Use

In developing guidelines for the use of drugs in treating hyperactivity, one needs to recognize several important factors in the preceding discussion and in Chapter 13 (Diagnosis of Hyperactivity). First, it is necessary to ensure that a child is indeed hyperactive before prescribing drug therapy. Although this seems somewhat simplistic, in actual practice this is not always done. Often, the diagnosis is not made by the physician involved with the child, but by parents or educators who are "fed up" with a problem child. This has led some clinicians (despite warnings in the literature) to believe in the sometimes hyperactive child, whose problem is supposedly organic but who does not show problems when in a doctor's office. It cannot be overemphasized here that if a child is only hyperactive some of the time, one is much more likely to be dealing with an emotional or behavioral problem, rather than an organic problem. It is the responsibility of a child's parents and teachers to *objectively* observe a child before pressuring a physician for a prescription that may make life more convenient for them rather than for the child.

Once a clear diagnosis of hyperactivity has been established, we must ensure that it is organically based. Is it accompanied by the pattern of symptoms likely to indicate a first or third unit disorder? Has the hyperactivity been present since birth or since a clearly defined brain insult? Is the hyperactivity seen at all times rather than just at home or school? Did the hyperactivity begin after an emotional trauma such as the loss of a parent or divorce? If, after examining all of these factors, one can conclude that we are dealing with a primary hyperactivity related to a possible brain dysfunction, then the child might be a possible candidate for drug therapy. If the above is done correctly, our experience suggests that about 50 percent or more of the hyperactive children (as labelled by parents or teachers) do not appear to be proper candidates for drug therapy.

At this point, one still needs to determine if alternate approaches might be successful without the use of drugs. Is the child's behavior at the point where it cannot be controlled by the use of behavior modification techniques (briefly described later in this chapter) or by changing the child's environment? Environmental changes might include a reduction of distractions for the child; more one-to-one contact with teachers' aides, volunteers, and parents; more opportunities to alternate periods of activity with periods of work; devising creative outlets for the child's energy (with his or her help) ; removing significant sources of frustration; using errorless and individualized teaching techniques; and so on. Behavior modification techniques can be used to reward the behavior desired of the child on a graduated basis and to remove rewards the child may obtain from his or her hyperactive behavior.

After the above considerations have been adequately confronted, then one may make a decision to try a child on one of the stimulant medications available for the treatment of hyperactivity. The child at this time should have a thorough medical workup to ensure that there are no physical problems which would interfere with the use of these medications. Parents should become familiar with the possible side effects of any medication suggested by their physician and the prevalence of those side effects. Ideally, there should be consultation with a physician, usually a psychiatrist or neurologist, who specializes in the behavior disorders of children.

Before any drug treatment is begun, the child should have a thorough psychoeducational examination in order to give a baseline level of intellectual abilities. This is important because we need to know if a drug is interfering with, aiding, or having no effect on the child's learning. Although many people believe that learning skills are improved, in some cases the only improvement may be a better attention span rather than improved learning skills (Millichap, Aymat, Sturgis, Iarsen, and Egan, 1968) . In some cases, there is a decrease in learning skills. By objectively assessing these abilities before and after the onset of drug usage, one can make much more intelligent decisions about the continuation of a drug.

After drug treatment is begun, one must take care to avoid long-term use which might impair height or weight gain in a growing child. Specifically, Safer and his associates (1972) suggest that the drug should not be given during weekends, school holidays, and other times when a higher energy level will not be a problem. This allows the child to get what educational benefits he or she can from the drug, while decreasing considerably the chances for any serious side effects. These periods (called drug holidays) are also useful in determining whether a child needs the drug or not. If the child's behavior does not significantly deteriorate when on such holidays, the child may no longer need the medication. If the child has become psychologically dependent on the medication and feels a need for it, drug holidays can be achieved by using placebos (inert pills with no effect which look like the real drug).

It is important to reemphasize here the role of the parent and the teacher. Since most physicians do not have the time to personally visit the home or the school, they will rely on the reports from the parents and teachers. These reports must be accurate and objective. It is easy to exaggerate a child's behavior when a teacher or parent is constantly harrassed by the inappropriate behavior of one child when there are often things that need to be accomplished. However, it is not in the child's best welfare to be on drugs when they are not needed and every effort should be made to ensure that this never occurs, no matter what the inconvenience or other price which must be paid.

The Child with Epilepsy

For the child with a significantly abnormal EEG suggesting the presence of seizures, the drugs of choice differ considerably from those normally prescribed for hyperactivity. Since seizures and hyperactivity may be related, it is important that this possibility be ruled out with a sleep and awake EEG in any child suspected of brain injury. Both sleep and awake EEGs should as a rule, be taken, as they often allow for a more sophisticated diagnosis.

Final Word on Drug Treatment

Before moving on to the question of behavior modification in hyperactivity, several points should be stressed to the reader. What has been written so far in this chapter represents guidelines. It is extremely important in the case of the individual child that one seeks out a physician who specializes in behavior disorders of children as well as other experts in the area who are available. The points presented here should be discussed with each of them. Educators should attempt to make such individuals available to parents, as well as to make sure that parents making such a decision about their child are aware of all of the factors involved. In this way, the most effective and considered use of these medications can be made and the possibilities of abuse and misuse avoided.

Behavior Modification

Behavior modification techniques are based on the assumption that we can change behavior by manipulating the consequences of behavior. By removing rewards, such as attention or getting out of an assignment, for inappropriate behavior and by providing rewards for behaviors we wish to encourge, such as staying in one place for ten minutes, the child's behavior may be changed so that it becomes more acceptable. Several studies have shown that these techniques can be effective in reducing hyperactive behavior no matter what their origin, although they are probably most effective for hyperactivity not due to brain injury in the first or third functional units. However, children with injuries to the second brain unit which results in secondary hyperactivity would probably be helped more by these methods than by medication.

An example of a behavior modification program for a hyperactive child was described by Patterson, Jones, Whittier, and Wright (1965). The authors observed two hyperactive children in a classroom, noting the occurrence of walking, talking, distraction, and wiggling. During the treatment phase, the authors rewarded one child with a sound after every time period in which the child did not show any of the above behaviors. The sound was a reward for the child because he had been previously taught that the sound meant he would later receive pennies and candy. The data from the treatment demonstrated that while the one child treated in this manner improved his behavior considerably, the other hyperactive child who did not receive the treatment failed to show any improvement.

Another important factor in addition to rewards for correct behavior is the removal of rewards the child may bet for his bad behavior. Sometimes these rewards are attention from the teacher. Undesired behavior can be eliminated by placing the child out of the classroom when he misbehaves. Another reward may be getting out of work. This can be resolved by not allowing a child to go home before all of his or her work is done, or arranging with parents to make sure the child will not get to see a favorite television program before all work for the day is completed.

In putting any of these programs together, one must always consider the principle of *shaping*. In shaping, one does not demand perfect behavior from the child right away, but only after a series of steps. For example, a child might be rewarded at first for "only three" disruptive behaviors in a given time period. Later, when the child is receiving regular awards, the rewards might come if there were "only two" disruptive incidents. Later this would be reduced to one and finally to none.

Shaping is extremely important as behavior modification programs will invariably fail if too much is demanded of a child too fast. Indeed, the desire to move ahead quickly and the expectations of instant success have sabotaged many behavior modification programs in the schools and at home. Combined with a proper analysis of a child's environment so that rewards may be given for desired behaviors and withdrawn for undesired behaviors, these techniques can be a powerful tool in controlling the hyperactive child.

Summary

The present chapter reviews treatments currently available for hyperactivity, concentrating on the medical treatment of the disorder. A survey of the literature indicates that drug treatment can be effective, but in only about 50 percent (or less) of the children labelled hyperactive by teachers and educators. In addition, drugs may have side effects such as loss of weight and cessation or limitation of growth. A set of guidelines for using drugs is suggested, including a strong diagnostic effort to ensure that the child has an organically based hyperactivity arising from injuries to the first or third functional units, the ones most likely to respond to drug treatment. The importance of attempting other treatment is emphasized, as well as a complete medical evaluation by a specialist in childhood behavior disorders. When drugs are used, drug holidays and constant reevaluation of the child's behavior are essential to avoid side effects and limit, as much as possible, the time the child is on the drug. The chapter also briefly describes the role of behavior modification techniques in controlling hyperactivity, emphasizing the importance of shaping techniques.

REFERENCES

Ackerman, P. T., Peters, J. E. and Dykman, R. A.: Children with specific
learning disabilities: Bender-Gestalt test findings and other signs. *J
Learn Disabil, 4:*437, 1971.

Annett, M.: Laterality of childhood hemiplegia and the growth of speech
and intelligence. *Cortex, 9:*4, 1973.

Ayers, F. W. and Torres, F.: The incidence of EEG abnormalities in a dyslexic and a control group. *J Clin Psychol, 23:*334, 1967.

Ayres, A. J.: Deficits in sensory integration in educationally handicapped
children. *J Learn Disabil, 2:*160, 1969.

Basser, L. S.: Hemiplegia of early onset and the faculty of speech with reference to the effects of hemispherectomy. *Brain, 85:*427, 1962.

Beery, J. W.: Matching of auditory and visual stimuli by average and retarded readers. *Child Dev, 38:*827, 1967.

Benton, A. L.: The fiction of the 'Gertsman Syndrome.' *J Neurol Neurosurg Psychiatry, 24:*176, 1961.

Benton, A. L.: Developmental aphasia and brain damage. *Cortex, 1:*40,
1964.

Benton, A. L.: Constructional apraxia and the minor hemisphere. *Confin
Neurol, 29:*1, 1967.

Benton, A. L.: Differential behavioral effects in frontal lobe disease. *Neuropsychologia, 6:*53, 1968.

Benton, A. L. and Bird, G. W.: The EEG and reading disability. *Am J
Orthopsychiatry, 33:*520, 1963.

Benton, A. L. and Fogel, M. L.: Three dimensional constructional praxis.
*Arch Neurol, 7:*347, 1962.

Benton, A. L., Hannay, J., and Varney, N. R.: Visual perception of line
direction in patients with unilateral brain disease. *Neurology, 25:*907,
1975.

Benton, A. L., Levin, H. S., and Van Allen, M. W.: Geographic orientation
in patients with unilateral cerebral disease. *Neuropsychologia, 12:*183,
1974.

Birch, H. G. and Belmont, L.: Auditory-visual integration in normal and
retarded readers. *Am J Orthopsychiatry, 34:*852, 1964.

Black, F. W.: Patterns of cognitive impairment in children with suspected and documented neurological dysfunction. *Percept Mot Skills, 39:*115, 1974.

Boll, T. J.: Psychological differentiation of patients with schizophrenia versus lateralized cerebrovascular, neoplastic, or traumatic brain disease. *J Abnorm Psychol, 83:*456, 1974.

Boll, T. J.: The effect of age at onset of brain damage on adaptive abilities in children. Unpublished manuscript, 1976.

Boll, T. J. and Reitan, R. M.: Motor and tactile-perceptual deficits in brain damaged children. *Percept Mot Skills, 34:*343, 1972.

Boll, T. J. and Reitan, R. M.: Effect of age on performance of the Trail Making test. *Percept Mot Skills, 36:*691, 1973.

Botez, M. I. and Wertheim, N.: Expressive aphasia and amusia following right frontal lesion in a right handed man. *Brain, 82:*186, 1959.

Bradley, C.: The behavior of children receiving benzedrine. *Am J Psychiatry, 94:*577, 1937.

Bradley, C.: Characteristics and management of children with behavioral problems associated with brain damage. *Pediatr Clin North Am, 4:*1049, 1957.

Brady, J. V. and Nauta, W. J.: Subcortical mechanisms in control of behavior. *J Comp Physiol Psychol, 48:*412, 1955.

Brain, W. R.: Visual orientation with special reference to lesions of the right cerebral hemisphere. *Brain, 64:*244, 1941.

Brewer, W. F.: Visual memory, visual encoding, and hemispheric localization. *Cortex, 5:*145, 1969.

Bruell, J. H. and Albee, G. W.: Higher intellectual functions in a patient with hemispherectomy for tumors. *J Consult Psychol, 26:*90, 1962.

Bryden, M. P.: Laterality effects in dichotic listening: relations with handedness and reading ability in children. *Neuropsychologia, 8:*443, 1970.

Burns, G. W. and Watson, B. L.: Factor analysis of the revised ITPA with underachieving children. *J Learn Disabil, 6:*371, 1973.

Capute, A. J., Niedermeyer, E. F., and Richardson, F.: The electroencephalogram in children with minimal cerebral dysfunction. *Pediatrics, 41:*1104, 1968.

Chess, S.: Diagnosis and treatment of the hyperactive child. *NY State J Med, 60:*2379, 1960.

Chusid, J.: *Correlative Neuroanatomy and Functional Neurology.* Los Altos, Lange, 1970.

Clements, S. D.: *Minimal Brain Dysfunction in Children: Terminology and Education.* Washington, Public Health Service (No. 1415), 1966.

Clements, S. D. and Peters, J. E.: Minimal brain dysfunctions in the school age child. *Arch Gen Psychiatry, 6:*185, 1962.

Cohn, R.: Delayed acquisition of reading and writing abilities in children. *Arch Neurol, 4:*153, 1961.

Connolly, C. J.: *External Morphology of the Primate.* Springfield, Thomas, 1950.

Corkin, S.: Tactually guided maze learning in man: Effects of unlateral cortical excisions and bilateral hippocampal lesions. *Neuropsychologia, 3:339,* 1965.

Crovitz, H. F. and Zener, K.: A group test for assessing hand and eye dominance. *Am J Psychol, 75:271,* 1962.

Croxer, M. E. and Lytton, H.: Reading disabilities and difficulties in finger localization and right-left discrimination. *Dev Psychol, 5:256,* 1971.

Czudner, A. and Rourke, B. P.: Simple reaction time in "brain damaged" and normal children under regular and irregular preparatory interval conditions. *Percept Mot Skills, 31:767,* 1970.

Czudner, A. and Rourke, B. P.: Age differences in visual reaction time of "brain damaged" and normal children under regular and irregular preparatory interval conditions. *J Exp Child Psychol, 13:516,* 1972.

Daryn, E.: Problems of children with "diffuse brain damage." *Arch Gen Psychiatry, 4:299,* 1960.

DeBoer, D. L., Kaufman, A. S., and McCarthy, D.: The use of the McCarthy scale in the identification, assessment, and deficit remediation of preschool and primary age children. Symposium presented at the meeting of the Council for Exceptional Children, New York, April, 1974.

Denckla, M. B.: Clinical syndromes in learning disabilities: The case for "splitting" versus "lumping." *J Learn Disabil, 5:401,* 1972.

Denhoff, E., Davids, A., and Hawkins, R.: Effects of dextroamphetamines on hyperkinetic children: A controlled double-blind study. *J Learn Disabil, 4:491,* 1971.

Drewe, E. A.: The effect of type and area of brain lesion on Wisconsin card sorting performance. *Cortex, 10:159,* 1974.

Eisenberg, L., Conners, C. K., and Sharpe, L. E.: A controlled study of the differential application of outpatient psychiatric treatment for children. *Jap J Child Psychiatry, 6:125,* 1965.

Elithorn, A., Piercy, M., and Crosskey, M. A.: Some mechanisms of tactile localization revealed by a study of leucotimized patients. *J Neurol Neurosurg Psychiatry, 15:272,* 1952.

Epstein, L. C., Lasagno, L., Conners, C. K., and Rodriguez, A.: A correlation of dextroamphetamine excretion and drug response in hyperkinetic children. *J Nerv Ment Dis, 146:136,* 1968.

Filskov, S. B. and Goldstein, S. G.: Diagnostic validity of the Halstead-Reitan neuropsychological battery. *J Consult Clin Psychol, 42:382,* 1974.

Finberg, E.: The normalizing effect of lateral amygdalar lesions upon the dorsomedial amygdalar symptoms in dogs. *Acta Neurobiol Exp, 33:449,* 1973.

Frantz, K. E.: Amnesia for left limbs and loss of interest and attention in left fields of vision. *J Nerv Ment Dis, 112:240,* 1950.

Frostig, M., Lefever, D. W., and Whittlesey, J. R. B.: A developmental test of visual perception for evaluating normal and neurologically handicapped children. *Percept Mot Skills, 12:383,* 1961.

Gaddes, W. H.: A neuropsychological approach to learning disorders. *J Learn Disabil, 1:*523, 1968.

Gainotti, G. and Tiacci, C.: The relationships between disorders of visual perception and unilateral spatial neglect. *Neuropsychologia, 9:*451, 1971.

Gastaut, H.: The role of the reticular formation in establishing conditioned reactions. In Jasper, K. H., Proctor, L. D., Knighton, R. S., Noshay, W. C. and Costello, R. C. (Eds.): *Reticular Formation of the Brain.* Boston, Little, 1958.

Gazzaniga, M. S.: Interhemispheric communication of visual learning. *Neuropsychologia, 4:*183, 1966.

Gazzaniga, M. S. and Sperry, R. W.: Language after section of the cerebral commissures. *Brain, 90:*131, 1967.

Geschwind, N.: Disconnexion syndromes in animals and man. *Brain, 88:* 237, 1965.

Geschwind, N.: Language and the brain. *Sci Am, 226:*76, 1972.

Ginsburg, G. P. and Hartwick, A.: Directional confusion as a sign of dyslexia. *Percept Mot Skills, 32:*535, 1971.

Golden, C. J.: The role of the psychologist in the rehabilitation of the neurologically impaired. *Professional Psychol, 8:*561, 1976.

Golden, C. J.: *Diagnosis and Rehabilitation in Clinical Neuropsychology.* Springfield, Thomas, 1978.

Gott, P. S.: Cognitive abilities following right and left hemispherectomy. *Cortex, 9:*266, 1973.

Guyer, B. L. and Friedman, M. P.: Hemispheric processing and cognitive styles in long-disabled and normal children. *Child Dev, 46:*658, 1975.

Hallahan, D. P. and Cruickshank, W. M.: *Psychoeducational Foundations of Learning Disabilities.* Englewood Cliffs, P-H, 1973.

Halstead, W. C.: *Brain and Intelligence.* Chicago, U of Chicago, 1947.

Hammill, D. O., Colarusso, J. L., and Wiederholt, J. L.: Diagnostic value of the Frostig test: A factor analytic approach. *J Spec Ed, 4:*279, 1970.

Hebb, D. O.: The effect of early and late brain injury upon test scores and the nature of normal adult intelligence. *Proc Am Philosoph Soc, 85:*275, 1942.

Hécaen, H., Ajuriaguerra, J., and Massonnet, J.: Les troubles visuo-constructifs par lésion parieto-occipitale droite. *Encephale, 40:*122, 1951.

Heimburger, R. F. and Reitan, R. M.: Easily administered written test for lateralizing brain lesions. *J Neurosurg, 18:*301, 1961.

Hertzig, M. F., Bortner, M., and Birch, H. G.: Neurologic findings in children educationally designated as "brain damaged." *Am J Orthopsychiatry, 39:*437, 1969.

Hinshelwood, J.: *Congenital Word-Blindness.* London, Lewis, 1917.

Huestos, R. D., Arnold, L. E. and Smeltzer, D. T.: Caffeine versus methylphenidata and d-amphetamine in minimal brain dysfunction: A double blind comparison. *Am J Psychiatry, 132:*868, 1975.

Hughes, J. R., Leander, J., and Ketchum, G.: Electroencephalographic study of specific reading disabilities. *Electroencephalogr Clin Neurophysiol, 1:* 277, 1949.

Hurwitz, I., Bibace, R. M., Wolff, P. H. and Rowbotham, B. M.: Neurophysiological function of normal boys, delinquent boys, and boys with learning problems. *Percept Mot Skills, 35:*387, 1972.

Hutt, S. J. and Hutt, C.: Hyperactivity in a group of epileptic (and some non-epileptic) brain-damaged children. *Epilepsia, 5:*334, 1964.

Ingram, T. T.: Soft signs. *Dev Med Child Neurol, 15:*527, 1973.

Isaacson, R. L.: *The Limbic System.* New York, Plenum, 1974.

Isaacson, R. L. and Kimble, D. P.: Lesions of the limbic system: Their effects upon hypotheses and frustration. *Behav Biol, 7:*767, 1972.

Jack, W. H. and Herbert, B. H.: Delayed auditory feedback and dyslexics. *J Educ Res, 68:*338, 1975.

Kalat, J. W.: Minimal brain dysfunction: Dopamine depletion? *Science, 194:*450, 1976.

Kaufman, A. S. and Kaufman, N. L.: *Clinical Evaluation of Young Children with the McCarthy Scales.* New York, Grune, 1977.

Kaufman, N. L. and Kaufman, A. S.: Comparison of normal and minimally brain dysfunctioned children on the McCarthy Scales of Children's Abilities. *J Clin Psychol, 30:*69, 1974.

Kawi, A. A. and Pasamanick, B.: Association factors of pregnancy with reading disorders in childhood. *JAMA, 166:*1420, 1958.

Kennard, M., Rabinowitch, R. D. and Wexler, D.: The abnormal electroencephalogram as related to learning disability in children. *Can Med Assoc J, 67:*330, 1952.

Keogh, B. K.: Hyperactivity and learning disorders: Review and speculations. *Except Child, 38:*101, 1971.

Kinsbourne, M. and Warrington, E. K.: Disorders of spelling. *J Neurol Neurosurg Psychiatry, 27:*224, 1964.

Kirk, S. A., McCarthy, J. J., and Kirk, W. D.: *Illinois Test of Psycholinguistic Abilities: Experimental Edition.* Urbana, U of Illinois, 1961.

Kirk, S. A., McCarthy, J. J. and Kirk, W. D.: *Illinois Test of Psycholinguistic Abilities, Revised Edition.* Urbana, U of Illinois, 1968.

Klonoff, H. and Low, M.: Disordered brain function in young children and early adolescents: Neuropsychological and electroencephalographic correlates. In Reitan, R. M. and Davison, L. A. (Eds.): *Clinical Neuropsychology: Current Status and Applications.* Washington, Winston Pr, 1974.

Klonhoff, H., Robinson, G. C., and Thompson, G.: Acute and chronic brain syndromes in children. *Dev Med Child Neurol, 11:*198, 1969.

Knobel, M.: Psychopharmacology for the hyperkinetic child. *Arch Gen Psychiatry, 6:*198, 1962.

Knobel, M., Wolman, B., and Mason, E.: Hyperkinesis and organicity in children. *Arch Gen Psychiatry, 1:*310, 1959.

Kohn, B. and Dennis, M.: Somatosensory functions after cerebral hemidecortication for infantile hemiplegia. *Neuropsychologia, 12:*119, 1974.

Koppitz, E. M.: *The Bender-Gestalt Test for Young Children.* New York, Grune, 1963.

Koppitz, E. M.: *The Bender-Gestalt Test for Young Children. Volume II.* New York, Grune, 1975.

Kramer, H. C.: Some observations in post-lobotomy patients. *J Nerv Ment Dis, 122:*89, 1955.

Lackner, J. R. and Teuber, H. L.: Alterations in auditory fusion thresholds after cerebral injury in man. *Neuropsychologia, 11:*409, 1973.

Lansdell, H.: Verbal and non-verbal factors in right-hemisphere speech: Relation to early neurological history. *J Comp Physiol Psychol, 69:*734, 1969.

Laufer, M. W., Denhoff, E. D., and Solomon, G.: Hyperkinetic impulse disorder in children's behavior problems. *Psychosom Med, 19:*38, 1957.

Leton, D. A.: Discriminant analysis of WISC profiles of learning-disabled and culturally disadvantaged pupils. *Psychology in the Schools, 9:*303, 1972.

Loeser, J. D. and Alvord, E. C.: Agenesis of the corpus callosum. *Brain, 91:*553, 1968.

Lucas, A. R., Rodin, E. A., and Simson, C. B.: Neurological assessment of children with early school problems. *Dev Med Child Neurol, 7:*145, 1965.

Luria, A. R.: *Restoration of Function After Brain Injury.* New York, Macmillan, 1963.

Luria, A. R.: *Higher Cognitive Functions in Man.* New York, Basic, 1966.

Luria, A. R.: *The Working Brain.* New York, Basic, 1973.

Luria, A. R., Pribram, H., and Homskaya, E. D.: An experimental analysis of the behavioral disturbance produced by a left frontal arachnoidal endothelioma (meningioma). *Neuropsychologia, 2:*257, 1964.

Lyle, J. G. and Goyen, J.: Performance of retarded readers on the WISC and educational tests. *J Abnorm Psychol, 74:*105, 1969.

McConnell, O. L.: Koppitz' Bender-Gestalt scores in relation to organic and emotional problems in children. *J Clin Psychol, 23:*370, 1967.

McFarland, J. N., Peacock, L. J., and Watson, J. A.: Mental retardation and activity level in rats and children. *Am J Ment Defic, 71:*376, 1966.

McFie, J.: The other side of the brain. *Dev Med Child Neurol, 12:*514, 1970.

McFie, J. and Zangwill, O. L.: Visual-constructive disabilities associated with lesions of the left cerebral hemisphere. *Brain, 83:*243, 1960.

McGlannan, F. K.: Familial characteristics of genetic dyslexia: Preliminary report from a pilot study. *J Learn Disabil, 1:*185, 1968.

McGrady, H. J. and Olson, D. A.: Visual and auditory learning processes in normal children and children with learning disabilities. *Except Child, 36:*581, 1970.

Malmo, H. P.: On frontal lobe functions: Psychiatric patient controls. *Cortex, 10:*231, 1974.

Masland, R. L.: Higher cerebral functions. *Ann Rev Physiol, 20:*522, 1958.

Mayo Clinic: *Clinical Examinations in Neurology.* Philadelphia, Saunders, 1976.

Meier, M. J. and French, L. G.: Lateralized deficits in complex visual discrimination and bilateral transfer of remininscence following unilateral temporal lobectomy. *Neuropsychologia, 3:*261, 1965.

Menkes, M., Rowe, J. S., and Menkes, J. H.: A twenty-five year follow-up study on the hyperkinetic child with minimal brain damage. *Pediatrics, 39:*393, 1967.

Mercer, C. D., Forgnone, C., and Wolking, W. D.: Definitions of learning disabilities used in the United States. *J Learn Disabil, 9:*376, 1976.

Millichap, J. G.: Drugs in the management of hyperkinetic and perceptually handicapped children. *JAMA, 206:*1527, 1968.

Millichap, J. G., Aymat, F., Sturgus, L. H., Larsen, K. W., and Egan, R. A.: Hyperkinetic behavior and learning disorders: LII. Battery of neuropsychological tests in controlled trial of methylphenidate. *Am J Dis Child, 116:*235, 1968.

Milner, B.: Effects of different brain lesions on card sorting. *Arch Neurol, 9:*90, 1963.

Milner, B.: Visually guided maze-learning in man: Effects of bilateral hippocampal, bilateral frontal, and unilateral cerebral lesions. *Neuropsychologia, 3:*317, 1965.

Milner, B.: Sparing of language functions after early unilateral brain damage. *Neurosci Res Program Bull, 12:*213, 1974.

Milner, B.: Psychological aspects of focal epilepsy and its neurological management. *Adv Neurol, 8:*299, 1975.

Milner, B. and Taylor, L.: Right hemisphere superiority in tactile pattern recognition after cerebral commissurotomy: Evidence for non-verbal memory. *Neuropsychologia, 10:*1, 1972.

Morgan, W. P.: A case of congenital word blindness. *Bri Med J, 2:*1612, 1896.

Muehl, S., Knott, J. R., and Benton, A. L.: EEG abnormality and psychological test performance in reading disability. *Cortex, 1:*434, 1965.

Myers, R. E.: Localization of function in the corpus callosum. *Arch Neurol, 1:*74, 1959.

Neff, W. D. and Goldberg, J. M.: Higher functions of the central nervous system. *Ann Rev Physiol, 22:*490, 1960.

Nonneman, A. J. and Isaacson, R. L.: Task dependent recovery after early brain damage. *Behav Biol, 8:*143, 1973.

Oettinger, L., Nekonishi, H., and Gill, I. G.: Cerebral dysrhythmia indiced by reading (subclinical reading epilepsy). *Dev Med Child Neurol, 9:*191, 1967.

Oldfield, R. C.: The assessment and analysis of handedness: The Edinburgh inventory. *Neuropsychologia, 9:*97, 1971.

Olson, V. and Johnson, C.: Structure and predictive validity of the Frostig Developmental test of visual perception in grades one and three. *J Spec Ed, 4:*49, 1970.

O'Neill, G. and Stanley, G.: Visual processing of straight lines in dyslexic and normal children. *Br J Educ Psychol, 46:*323, 1976.

Osmon, D., Sweet, J., and Golden, C. J.: Rhythm and aphasia deficits in unilateral left hemisphere injuries. *Int J Neuroscience,* in press, 1978.

Ounsted, C.: The hyperactive syndrome in epileptic children. *Lancet, 269:* 303, 1955.

Papez, J. W.: Path for projection of impulses to the cortex. *Dis Nerv Syst, 17:*103, 1956.

Papez, J. W.: Visceral brain, its component parts, and their connections. *J Nerv Ment Dis, 126:*40, 1958.

Pasamanick, B. and Knobloch, H.: Syndrome of minimal brain damage in infancy. *JAMA, 170:*1384, 1959.

Penfield, W. and Mathieson, G.: Memory. *Arch Neurol, 31:*145, 1974.

Penfield, W. and Milner, B.: Memory deficit produced by bilateral lesions in the hippocampal zone. *Arch Neurol Psychiatry, 79:*479, 1958.

Penn, J. M.: Reading disabilities: A neurological deficit? *Except Child, 33:*243, 1966.

Peters, J. E., Romine, J. S., and Dykman, R. A.: A special neurological examination of children with learning disabilities. *Dev Med Child Neurol, 17:*63, 1975.

Pribam, K. H. and Bagshaw, M.: Further analysis of the temporal lobe syndrome utilizing frontotemporal ablations. *J Comp Neurol, 99:*347, 1953.

Pyfer, J. L. and Carlson, B. R.: Characteristic motor development of children with learning disabilities. *Percept Mot Skills, 35:*291, 1972.

Ramier, A. M. and Hecaen, H.: Role respectif des atteintes frontales et de de la latéralisation lesionelle dans les déficits de la "fluence verbale." *Rev Neurol, 123:*17, 1970.

Reed, J. C.: Reading achievement as related to differences between WISC verbal and performance IQ's. *Child Dev, 38:*835, 1967.

Reitan, R. M.: A research program on the psychological effects of brain lesions in human beings. In Ellis, N. R. (Ed.): *International Review of Research in Mental Retardation, Volume I.* New York, Acad Pr, 1966.

Reitan, R. M.: Psychological effects of cerebral lesions in children of early school age. In Reitan, R. M. and Davison, L. A. (Eds.): *Clinical Neuropsychology: Current Status and Application.* Washington, Winston, 1974.

Reitan, R. M. and Davison, L. A.: *Clinical Neuropsychology: Current Status and Applications.* Washington, Winston, 1974.

Rossi, A. O.: Genetics of learning disabilities. *J Learn Disabil, 5:*489, 1972.

Rourke, B. P.: Brain-behavior relationships in children with learning disabilities: A research program. *Am Psychol, 30:*911, 1975.

Rourke, B. P. and Czudner, A.: Age differences in auditory reaction time of "brain damaged" and normal children under regular and irregular preparatory interval conditions. *J Exp Child Psychol, 14:*372, 1972.

Rourke, B. P., Dietrich, D. M., and Young, G. C.: Significance of WISC verbal-performance discrepancies for younger children with learning disabilities. *Percept Mot Skills, 36:*275, 1973.

Rourke, B. P. and Telegdy, G. A.: Lateralizing significance of WISC verbal performance discrepancies for older children with learning disabilities. *Percept Mot Skills, 33:*875, 1971.

Rourke, B. P., Yanni, D. W., MacDonald, G. W., and Young, G. C.: Neuropsychological significance of lateralized deficits on the Grooved Pegboard test for older children with learning disabilities. *J Consult Clin Psychol, 41:*128, 1973.

Rourke, B. P., Young, G. C., and Flewelling, R. W.: The relationship between WISC verbal-performance discrepancies and selective verbal, auditory-perceptual, visual-perceptual, and problem solving abilities in children with learning disabilities. *J Clin Psychol, 27:*475, 1971.

Russell, W. R. and Espir, M. L. E.: *Traumatic Aphasia.* London, Oxford, 1961.

Sabatino, D. A. and Becker, J. T.: Relations among five basic tests of behavior. *Percept Mot Skills, 29:*487, 1969.

Safer, D., Allen, R., and Barr, E.: Depression of growth in hyperactive children on stimulant drugs. *N Engl J Med, 287:*217, 1972.

Sanides, F.: Structure and function of the human frontal lobe. *Neuropsychologia, 2:*209, 1964.

Sattler, J. M.: *Assessment of Children's Intelligence.* Philadelphia, Saunders, 1974.

Sauguet, J., Benton, A. L., and Hecaen, H.: Disturbances of the body schema in relation to language impairment and hemispheric locus of lesion. *J Neurol Neurosurg Psychiatry, 34:*496, 1971.

Scoville, W. B. and Milner, B.: Loss of recent memory after bilateral hippocampal lesions. *J Neurol Neurosurg Psychiatry, 20:*11, 1957.

Shaywitz, B. A.: Minimal brain dysfunction: Dopamine depletion? *Science, 194:*452, 1976.

Shipley, T. and Jones, R. W.: Initial observations on sensory interaction and the theory of dyslexia. *J Commun Disorders, 2:*295, 1969.

Sleator, E. and Von Neumann, A.: Methylphenidate in the treatment of the hyperkinetic child. *Clin Pediatr, 13:*19, 1974.

Smith, A.: Neuropsychological testing in neurological disorders. *Adv Neurol, 7:*49, 1975.

Smith, A.: *Differing Effects of Hemispherectomy in Children and Adults.* Paper presented to the 84th annual convention of the American Psychological Association, Washington, D. C., 1976.

Sprague, R. L., Barnes, K. R., and Werry, J. S.: Methylphenidate and thiorodazine: learning, reaction time, activity and classroom behavior in disturbed children. *Am J Orthopsychiatry, 40:*615, 1970.

Spring, C. and Capps, C.: Encoding speeds, rehearsals, and probed recall of dyslexic boys. *J Educ Psychol, 66:*780, 1974.

Stavrianos, B. K.: Can projective test measures aid in the detection and differential diagnosis of reading deficits. *J Project Techniq Personal Assess, 35:*80, 1971.

Steinberg, G. G., Troshinsky, C., and Steinberg, H. R.: Dextroamphetamine responsive behavior disorders in school children. *Am J Psychiatry, 128:* 174, 1971.

Symonds, C.: Disorders of memory. Brain, *89:*625, 1966.

Taylor, A. M. and Warrington, E. K.: Visual discrimination in patients with localized cerebral lesions. *Cortex, 9:*82, 1973.

Wada, J. A., Clarke, R., and Hamm, A.: Cerebral hemispheric assymetry in humans. *Arch Neurol, 32:*239, 1975.

Wagner, E. E. and Murray, A.: Bender-Gestalt of organic children: Accuracy of clinical judgement. *J Proj Techniq Person Assess, 33:*240, 1969.

Waugh, R. P.: The ITPA: Ballast or bonanza for the school psychologist. *J School Psychol, 13:*201, 1975.

Werry, J. S.: Developmental hyperactivity. *Pediatr Clin North Am, 15:*581, 1968.

Werry, J. S., Weiss, G., Douglas, V., and Martin, J.: Studies on the hyperactive child. *J Am Acad Child Psychiatry, 5:*292, 1966.

Wiig, E. H. and Semele, E. M.: Productive language abilities in learning disabled adolescents. *J Learn Disabil, 8:*578, 1975.

Wikler, A. W., Dixon, J. F., and Parker, J. B.: Brain function in problem children and controls: Psychometric, neurological, and electroencephalographic comparisons. *Am J Psychiatry, 127:*634, 1970.

Zaidel, D. and Sperry, R. W.: Performance on Raven's progressive matrices test by subjects with cerebral commissurotomy. *Cortex, 9:*34, 1973.

Zurif, E. B. and Carson, G.: Dyslexia in relation to cerebral dominance and temporal analysis. *Neuropsychologia, 8:*351, 1970.

Zurif, E. B. and Ramier, A. M.: Some effects of unilateral brain damage on the perception of dichotically presented phoneme sequences and digits. *Neuropsychologia, 10:*103, 1972.

AUTHOR INDEX

SUBJECT INDEX